OTHER BOOKS BY JULIET F. BRUDNEY

JANUS: *A Study of Forced Relocation of Older People*

OTHER BOOKS BY HILDA SCOTT

DOES SOCIALISM LIBERATE WOMEN? *Experiences from Eastern Europe*

SWEDEN'S "RIGHT TO BE HUMAN:" *Sex-Role Equality, the Goal and the Reality*

Ed. with Margrit Eichler, WOMEN IN FUTURES RESEARCH

WORKING YOUR WAY TO THE BOTTOM: *The Feminization of Poverty*

FORCED OUT

When Veteran Employees are Driven from Their Careers

JULIET F. BRUDNEY
and HILDA SCOTT

A FIRESIDE BOOK
PUBLISHED BY SIMON & SCHUSTER, INC.
NEW YORK

Copyright © 1987 by Juliet F. Brudney and Hilda Scott

A Fireside Book
Published by Simon & Schuster, Inc.
Simon & Schuster Building
Rockefeller Center
1230 Avenue of the Americas
New York, New York 10020
FIRESIDE and colophon are registered trademarks of Simon &
Schuster, Inc.

Designed by Stanley S. Drate/Folio Graphics Co. Inc.

Manufactured in the United States of America

10 9 8 7 6 5 4 3 2 1

Library of Congress Cataloging in Publication Data

Brudney, Juliet F.
  Forced out.

  "A Fireside book"
  Bibliography: p.
  Includes index.
  1. Age and employment—United States. 2. Age
discrimination in employment—United States.
3. Career changes—United States. I. Scott, Hilda,
date. II. Title.
HD6280.B78 1987   650.1'4'0240564   87-14927
ISBN 0-671-64422-4
ISBN 0-671-64411-4 (pbk.)

To the men and women who shared
their job-keeping and job-seeking
experiences with us,
with gratitude and admiration

CONTENTS

ACKNOWLEDGMENTS

The understanding and cooperation of numerous institutions and individuals combined to make this book possible. The authors would like to express their sincere appreciation to the staffs of the following organizations in the Greater Boston area, who helped to put us in touch with many of the men and women whom we interviewed, and who patiently answered our numerous questions: ABLE (Ability Based on Long Experience), Civil Liberties Union of Massachusetts, Greater Boston Legal Services, Jewish Vocational Services, Keystone Associates, Massachusetts Commission Against Discrimination, Massachusetts Office of Elder Affairs, Massachusetts Division of Employment Security, Minuteman Home Care Corperation, National Association for the Advancement of Colored People, Quincy *Patriot Ledger*, Radcliffe Career Services, Radcliffe Institute, Radcliffe Seminars, Right Associates, Somerville Cambridge Elder Services, Transitional Employment Enterprises, Two/Ten Foundation, Villers Foundation, Widening Horizons, the Women's Educational and Industrial Union, and the Women's Job Counseling Center.

Thanks are also due to the American Association of Retired Persons, the Older Women's League, the U.S. Senate Special Committee on Aging, and the Women's Research and Education Institute in Washington, D.C.; as well as the Community Council of Greater New York and Lee Hecht Associates in New York.

We particularly want to acknowledge the assistance of Elizabeth Bartholet, Robin Battista, William Cara-Donna, Paula Doress, U.S. Congressman Barney Frank, Nina Gaetjens, Stephen McConnell, Terry Morris, Judith Podell, Glendora Putnam, Paula Rayman, Sara E. Rix, Allan R. Rosenberg, Anna Shenk, Muriel Snowden, Phyllis Stein, and George Zeller.

We owe a special debt of gratitude to Harriet F. Pilpel, who guided us across that crucial bridge between grand ideas and publishing reality with wise advice and kind words of encouragement.

We are deeply grateful to Cathy Hemming, the publisher of Fireside Books, who discovered our book and supported it unfailingly.

Finally, thanks go to our skilled and tactful editor, Herbert Schaffner, whose feeling for the right word added much to the final product.

FOREWORD

The genesis of our book can be traced to a series of experiences that began shortly after I undertook to write a column called "Living with Work" for the *Boston Globe* in 1980. I used a letter-answering format, and I began getting letters from people who had job problems because the federal government and the state were cutting back, and Massachusetts was deep in recession.

At first the letters came from so-called problem groups: re-entry women, or young women in jobs they hated, or women in professions who were facing sex barriers or child care problems. I heard from blacks and Hispanics who were experiencing discrimination, and also from people with physical and other disabilities, reformed alcoholics and former prisoners. The word *old* never appeared.

After some months I noticed that I was receiving an increasing number of letters from men and women in their late 50s and early 60s asking me for ideas on how to get a decent full-time job. I thought, mistakenly as it turned out, that it would be relatively easy to help them. I knew that there were community agencies set up specifically to find employment for that age group. I called one of these in Cambridge, where I live.

The woman I spoke to said yes, that was their purpose; but because the agency was supported by government funds, there were certain restrictions. They could serve clients 55 and over in a particular geographic area only, provided they were low income. She could advise me on a case-by-case basis, or I could refer my letter-writers to her and she would do her best. But, she said, there was no general program to help older people get jobs. Finally, she told me that most of the people who came to the agency wanted part-time work.

None of the people who had written to me wanted part-time jobs. They were engineers, sales managers, social workers. They all wanted full-time jobs with a steady income and benefits. Some indicated that they would take part-time work as a last resort. I began to print their letters and my answers. In the course of trying to help these men and women, I got to know people at other agencies. Everyone had the same income and geographic restrictions. When I read them a letter, I was told that they really could not help mid-level people. They simply did not have access to the kind of jobs these people were looking for. They were serving low-skill workers over 55, and retired persons who wanted to supplement their income without having their social security benefits cut. (That meant, in 1982, that if they were under 70 their earnings could not total more than $6,000 a year.)

I went along with the system, always unable to help certain readers but getting to know the agencies better, including several career counseling agencies that had special programs for older people, without income or residence restrictions, serving unemployed professionals. The director of one of these was the first to say that mid-level workers were indeed in a serious situation, that they were not going to get other jobs unless they were willing to scale down their salary demands.

It had taken me all that time to realize that there was a big problem out there that I hadn't seen reported in the newspapers. I started to write about it in my column. I began getting many more letters saying yes, there is a problem, and I'm part of it.

In 1983 Operation ABLE, modeled after an organization that had started in Chicago to expand opportunities for older workers through cooperation with business, government and community organizations, began service in Boston. I met the people there, and I discussed the problem at length with the executive director. His position was that some companies were beginning to do something about the problem, that these pioneers would be role models, and more and more firms would follow their example.

It was a matter of good business, he said. The message to forward-looking entrepreneurs was: America is aging. The pool of young people you want to draw on is getting smaller and smaller, and all these richly experienced older workers are available to you. It is ridiculous not to take advantage of them. You are going to need them, so begin now and set up a program, as Travelers Insurance and some other companies are doing.

In May 1985 a large national conference on aging was held in San Francisco. It promised a whole day devoted to employment opportunities for older workers, including those with professional training and experience. I was extremely interested, and decided to write a column on the conference and interview four or five speakers by telephone before it took place.

The conversations were disappointing. What they

had to tell me did not reflect great strides forward with respect to the number of people served or the level of jobs. The companies these speakers represented had various programs designed to bring back retired people. Some were temporary projects employing full-time professional workers, which was fine except that the number of people involved was very small.

The larger number of people were being re-employed as temporary clericals by Travelers Insurance and some other companies—a bank in Chicago, for example, and a large company in Florida.

At the conference itself there were additional speakers on employment issues. I didn't hear anything but the now familiar refrain: We must remember, the demographics are such that we are going to need to bring people back from retirement. And when the time comes we are not going to be able to find them and train them. So this is the time to get the mechanism and the movement going.

A representative of Bank of America talked at length about how important it was to make that company policy, and how, after many meetings, the bank was united on it from "top to bottom." I went up to the speaker afterwards and asked to interview some beneficiaries of this policy for my column. She told me that the policy had not yet been put into practice, so there was no evidence that anything was really going to happen.

The only people who reported any concrete results were on an afternoon panel on the elderly market. Motel chains, Sears, and other companies talked about why and how they cultivated elderly consumers, and they had indeed, with sales and profit figures to show it.

I came to the conclusion that the problem of older job-seekers were simply not being addressed. About that time articles started to appear, not about how hard it was for experienced older workers to find jobs, but about how many older people in the professional, managerial, and technical category were being thrown out of work. Companies had been making use of early retirement programs as a cost-cutting measure for years, offering special severance or pension benefits to older executives to persuade them to leave before pension age. Some important age discrimination cases, where managers or other skilled personnel were terminated for no other reason than that they were over 50, were fought in the 1970s. Now these "golden handshake" programs were multiplying and affecting mid-level people. The media began to take notice.

What interested me was not just that certain companies were trying to shed some corporate fat, but that these people, and others who were laid off without "exit incentives," could not seem to get back into the labor market. The main targets of these publicized early retirement programs in the business world were men, and the reason was obvious. Women in the middle and upper age brackets had hardly penetrated these upper salary reaches.

I believe that it took me so long to recognize the extent of the problem because it was never a surprise to me that older women with training and experience had difficulty finding a decent position. I always had, myself. Or that older women lost jobs because younger women and men were preferred. It was just as horrible for them as for men, but they were better prepared for shock. It was definitely a big surprise to me to receive so many appeals from white, middle-class, mid-level men. I had never thought of them as being in trouble. It did not occur to me that age was going to lick them.

Obviously there were many more issues to be explored than could be aired in a newspaper column. As a member of the generation concerned, the subject was of more than passing interest to me. I suggested to my friend and fellow older-worker, Hilda Scott, who also writes on work related subjects, and with whom I frequently discussed social policy problems, that we investigate it together. The following pages are the result.

JULIET F. BRUDNEY

Cambridge, Massachusetts
March, 1987

INTRODUCTION

This book is about the occupational risks of being over 50 years old. It will expose age discrimination in its many guises. If you have experienced one or more of them, you will discover how others in your situation have responded. You will also find in it some practical guidelines for recovering your career in today's work world.

When we decided to write a book about the job discrimination suffered by older mid-level workers, we agreed that we wanted to base it on their experiences, not on statistics and generalizations. There are studies of older workers designed for academics and policy makers; but until our study, no one had written a book for the general public about the problems older people face when they lose their jobs and must look for others.

We interviewed more than 100 men and women between the ages of 50 and 70 with tested skills in mid-level jobs. We have used many of their stories, told largely in their own words, to shed light on how older

Americans who have ability and really want to work fare in the present job environment. Whenever conversation has turned on our work-in-progress, people have said: "That's my father's story"; or "You're talking about my mother"; or "Maybe I ought to call my brother-in-law and see how he's doing." The problem is widespread and growing.

But aren't good jobs as scarce for many other Americans: for young people; for minorities; for women reentering the work force; for production workers in the auto, steel, oil, and other declining industries? Why, then, write a book about mature men and women who are assumed to be at the peak of their careers—jobs better than most at salaries higher than average, enviably placed in that occupational classification known to government statisticians as "professional/management/ technical"?

What happens to older professional, managerial, and other mid-level workers may seem to touch only one-quarter of the American work force directly, but we believe that it carries a message for everyone about the fate of the American Dream. It promises that if you work hard, show initiative, don't make too many waves, and save your money, you will progress up the ladder and spend your latter years in security. The men and women who are seen falling off the ladder in this book, entered the work force shortly after the victory for democracy in World War II gave new content to the dream. They followed all the rules, yet their experiences tell us that it's time to stop dreaming.

■ ■ ■

Writing this book, we have read the studies, surveys, analyses and other texts which the reader will find listed in the bibliography. The facts and figures reflect conflicting trends, giving rise to more than one paradox.

The "greying" of America is part of a general phenomenon in the industrially developing world. The American population has been steadily aging since the beginning of the century, thanks to improved life expectancy and a generally declining birthrate. In the United States, this trend is about to take a big leap forward: The baby-boom generation born between 1946 and 1962, is turning 40. Beginning in 1990 the population aged 45 and over will increase markedly. At the same time, younger age groups will be decreasing. While in 1910 one in ten American was over 55; today the figure is one in five. In 2010 it will be about one in four.

First Paradox

An aging population is not an aging work force. Although Americans are staying fit longer, and jobs are less strenuous, people are retiring earlier. Only 30 percent of jobs today are in the physically demanding fields of mining, manufacturing, transport and agriculture. Yet the participation of men over 65 in the labor force (the number of people working or looking for work) has dropped over three decades from 46 percent in 1950 to 19 percent in 1980. More than two-thirds of retiring Americans apply for social security before they are 65. Today only two-thirds of men aged 55 to 64 are employed. Government statisticians predict that in 20 years, when the oldest baby boomers are entering their 60s, only one out of two men in this age group will be in the work force.

Short of a massive program to create jobs, nothing will staunch this flow. Between 1983 and 1995 alone, ten million additional men and nearly fourteen million more women aged 35 to 54 will have joined the labor force, putting heavy pressure on the supply of jobs. Even if the 55–64 age group makes some employment gains, its labor force participation measured in percent will drop as the baby boomers pass age 55 and the group swells in size.

Second Paradox

Institutionalized policies and pressures have encouraged older Americans to retire at ever-earlier ages. And now older Americans are being accused of knocking off work and enjoying a high standard of living at the taxpayer's expense.

A major purpose of the Social Security Act of 1935 setting retirement at 65, and of subsequent amendments permitting early retirement at 62 and expanding the law's coverage, was to get older workers off the market and make room for the young. All social historians agree on this. Social Security set the norm for civil service retirement policies and for the pension schemes designed by business in recent decades, many of which had mandatory retirement provisions. By 1975 private pension plans allowing retirement at age 55 outnumbered those beginning at age 60.

These measures helped to reduce the official poverty rate among older Americans from 34 percent in 1960 to 12.4 percent in 1984, and relieved their children and grandchildren of much of the financial responsibility for their care. They also reinforced existing stereotypes about the waning powers of the middle-aged and contributed to creating a work environment hostile to grey hairs and wrinkles.

Then in the 1980s, with the advent of an administration determined to cut federal spending, the human services were the target of choice. Concerns about the high cost of Social Security led to generalized attacks on the elderly as fat-cats living off the younger, working generations. Articles like "The Coming Conflict as We Soak the Young to Enrich the Old," published in the *Washington Post* in January, 1986, and widely reprinted, helped to give the myth currency. The fact that 40 percent of households headed by a person of 65 or over had incomes below $15,000 in 1984, compared to 20 percent of younger families, or that nearly half the elderly contribute money to their children or grandchildren received less media exposure.

Third Paradox

While the number of available younger workers is shrinking, older workers, who should be gaining in popularity, are losing their jobs at an increasingly early age. When we set out to discover what difficulties older workers who did not want to retire were experiencing, we were surprised to find ourselves talking to many people in their early and mid-50s, some even younger. Their problem is not whether to work up to or beyond retirement age, but how to get near retirement age with the option of whether or not to retire still intact!

Much is made of Americans' haste to retire and the high degree of satisfaction retirement brings them. There is just as much evidence that many more older workers would prefer to continue working if they had the chance. Findings vary widely, according to Stanford University Law School Professor Lawrence Friedman. "There seems to be no agreement whatsoever on the number of workers who want to stay on the job. . . . Probably many workers are unsure themselves why they retire."

The most comprehensive study, by Herbert S. Parnes and other scholars for the Center for Human Resource Research at Ohio University, is a survey that followed the attitudes of a representative sample of men from

1966 to 1981, where the 2700 men remaining were age 60 to 74. Its major message is that the majority of retirements are voluntary.

The figures can be read differently, however. One-quarter of the sample had not retired. Of those who had, one-third retired for health reasons and at least 10 percent because of loss of job and lack of job opportunities. Consequently, of the entire sample of men aged 60 to 74, only about 40 percent had retired wholly voluntarily. Some of them continued to work after retirement.

The Parnes study was made before the current explosion of early retirement offers, to be discussed more fully below and in Chapter One, which raises new questions about the meaning of "voluntary." How voluntary is retirement when the alternatives are to take the money and run, or stick around and risk seeing one's job disappear a year from now when no rewards for leaving quietly are offered?

Like all major studies of older workers, the Parnes survey deals with men only, and this skews the overall picture badly. Women are responsible for almost the entire increase in the work force of people over the age of 45 that has taken place in the past 35 years. Women now make up 40 percent of the older work force, compared to 19 percent in 1950; and the figure will rise to 44 percent in 1996.

Contrary to the trend among older men, more and more women aged 55 to 64 are working. Their labor force participation has risen from 27 percent in 1950 to 42 percent in 1984. The explanations given include women's lower salaries, resulting in lower social security benefits; the small percentage of typical women's jobs covered by private pension plans; and the large number of older women living alone, dependent entirely on their own income.

A less comprehensive but more recent study, which

does include women, was made by the American Association of Retired Persons in 1985. This survey of 1,500 older Americans revealed that of those employed, 79 percent of women and 72 percent of men wanted to remain in the labor force. Desire to work correlated with occupational status and income. A large majority of salaried workers preferred to work, while only 35 percent of lower level blue-collar employees wanted to continue after retirement age. Of those already in retirement, two out of five said they would rather be working.

Is a change visible on the horizon? Will employers welcome older people as younger ones become scarcer? According to a nationwide survey of 400 corporations made by Yankelovich, Skelley and White in the mid-1980s, workers over 50 are valued for their experience, knowledge and work habits. Most surprising, employers consider them cost effective. Their higher salaries and benefits are balanced by their extra value to the company. They get high marks for productivity, commitment to quality, and performance. These favorable opinions have been confirmed by numerous research studies which find older workers scoring as well or better than the average for younger ones on such traits as creativity, flexibility, facility of information processing, absenteeism, and turnover.

While this may be the official view of some companies, there is little evidence that managers, personnel officers and others who make employment decisions are actually changing their policies accordingly. The business environment has been less than enthusiastic about creating employment opportunities for older workers despite the coming shortage of younger ones. This is especially true when it comes to experienced professional, managerial, and technical people.

The National Older Workers Information System (NOWIS), a computerized system for the collection of information about company programs for workers over 50, has been developed at the University of Michigan. According to the latest NOWIS report, its database in September 1984 included 180 companies with 369 programs or practices for older workers, the majority concerned with hiring, training, retirement planning, job redesign, or flexible scheduling. Only 9 percent, or a total of 34, involved hiring older workers for full-time jobs. Most of these involve a small number of experts with scarce skills, or a larger number of older workers who have been taken on in entry-level jobs.

According to the report, "there is a disproportionately high representation of programs for clerical workers–particularly part-time arrangements," among the programs. Travelers Insurance's much publicized job bank, considered a model for other companies, is one of these. Travelers maintains a pool of retirees from which it draws receptionists, typists, messengers, data-entry operators, and accountants as needed, for a maximum of 40 hours a month.

Travelers saves by not having to pay overtime to regular employees, and by avoiding the 30–50 percent markup that commercial temporary agencies charge. While such programs may be a boon to some workers and to companies, they do not answer the needs of skilled mid-level workers over 50.

All the evidence points towards fewer opportunities in the future for such people. In the radical restructuring that is taking place in the U.S. economy as it shifts from a manufacturing to a service base, a million-and-a-half manufacturing jobs were lost between 1980 and 1985 alone. According to government sources, older workers are a disproportionate number of the long-term unemployed resulting from these layoffs. They are more likely than younger ones to become discouraged and stop looking for work. That means that after twenty-eight days they are no longer counted in unemployment statistics.

Managerial and technical staff are affected as well as line workers. Ford Motor Company, for example, has announced that it will reduce its salaried work force by 10,000 before 1990. Across-the-board cutbacks are taking place in high technology companies as well. AT&T, which laid off 53,000 people between 1984 and 1986, declared that it would terminate 27,400 employees in 1987, including 10,400 managerial workers.

In addition to wholesale work-force reductions that force out both young and old workers, layoffs specifically targetted at older workers are gaining momentum across the country. These programs, using "exit incentives," began to gain popularity in the mid-1970s, as a way of terminating higher salaried older employees in preference to lower paid younger ones without violating the federal Age Discrimination in Employment Act. "Voluntary" early retirement schemes offer "golden handshakes"—or as some people call them, "golden shoves"—to employees who save the company money by leaving before their time.

A few top executives receive "golden parachutes" in the form of a six-figure lump sum. For most, however, the lure is an early pension with added service credits; often there is a cash incentive as well. The way this practice works is described in detail in Chapter Two.

It is estimated that 600,000 mid-level white-collar positions were eliminated by using "exit incentives" between 1980 and 1986, including 11,200 jobs at Du Pont and 6,000 at Atlantic Richfield in 1985; and 2,000 at CBS, 7,500 at Motorola, 3,800 at Monsanto Chemical, 4,000 at Union Carbide, and 10,000 at IBM in 1986.

Smaller numbers of employees were affected at hundreds of other companies. Pratt & Whitney, jet engine builders, scheduled layoffs for 1,500–2,000 in 1987; John

Hancock Mutual Insurance offered its "special opportunities arrangement" to some 1,500 employees.

This wave of "fat-trimming" has been intensified by fear of corporate takeovers. Firms become mean and lean to increase profitability and drive up their stock prices before a raiding corporation comes in and does it for them.

While these measures are applauded on Wall Street, economists point out that the long-run cost of unemployment benefits, Social Security taxes, loss of purchasing power, and loss of talent may outweigh the short-term gains. Economics writer Robert Kuttner has dubbed this practice "casino economy," gambling on quick financial advantage that has nothing to do with quality of work force or product.

There are few new openings for the mid-level, middle-aged people washed ashore by these waves of layoffs. While there was an impressive net increase of seven million in the total number of jobs in the U.S. between 1979 and 1984, the labor force grew by nine million in the same period, resulting in an increase of two million unemployed. Just as important for job seekers hoping for mid-range salaries, a study of federal employment data made for the Joint Economic Committee of Congress and released in 1986 reveals that 60 percent of the new positions are service jobs, paying less than $7,000 a year. In the same period, the total of U.S. jobs paying more than $14,000 declined by 1.8 million and those paying more than $28,000 by 7 percent.

Today unemployed older workers are competing with younger workers for mid-level jobs and meeting with age discrimination for the second time. While their original problem may have been the size of their paycheck, the current obstacles are harder to identify. Federal and state legislation has outlawed age discrimination in hiring, and in 1986 Congress put an end to mandatory retirement for all but a few jobs. So far these changes have merely driven discrimination underground. The myths about age, and just plain prejudice, are alive and well—as we will see in the following pages.

A number of scholarly studies have been made in recent years about the future of America's greying workers. But there is no consensus on how the far-reaching changes we have mentioned—in the economy, the population structure, the perception of age, and employer responses—will come together.

If we want to influence this future for the national good, and this would mean at the very least preventing the further marginalization of capable older people, we first need a wider public understanding of what is happening right now. Our purposes in this book are several:

- To help bring to public attention the policies, pressures, and stereotypes that combine to force older mid-level workers out of their careers;
- To assure professionals, managers, technicians, and other skilled white-collar personnel who are over 50 and looking for a job—or who fear that they may soon find themselves without one—that the most serious obstacles they face are not of their own making. Their experiences are shared by many, many others. We offer some strategies that have worked in cases with which we are familiar;
- To warn these men and women that career life after 50 will continue to be at risk unless those whose interests are at stake get together and press publicly and persistently for institutional action;
- To propose some practical steps that older workers and the agencies interested in helping them can take to improve the situation;

In Chapter One we take a brief look at the women and men we talked to: how we came to know them and some of their characteristics as a group.

In Chapters Two through Five we let them tell how they lost their jobs, what happened when they tried to find new ones, and their experiences with the machinery that has been set up to give them legal protection against age discrmination. Four more chapters present some typical outcomes: failures, concessions, compromises, and some real comebacks. The final chapter presents our conclusions and proposals.

1 | THE PLACE AND THE PLAYERS

The Massachusetts economy was booming in 1985 when we began to talk about writing this book. The Help Wanted sections of the *Sunday Boston Globe* ran to eighty pages. The recession that had hit the state in the late 1970s had given way to an upswing, and the unemployment rate was half the national average. With high technology in the lead, the demand for workers at all levels was swelling. Many companies offered employees a cash bounty for suggesting a candidate who accepted a position.

This was not true in all sectors. Traditional industries, like metal-working, shipbuilding, shoes, and textiles, were in a slump; and the human services sector was suffering from federal cutbacks. Some regions had relatively high unemployment. But in the state as a whole job opportunities were multiplying; and the Boston metropolitan area, where one-half the state's labor force is employed, was thriving.

If, as we knew to be the case, older men and women who were trying to re-establish their professional, technical or management careers were encountering barriers to employment, greater Boston was an ideal place to find out why. By examining their job-hunting and job-finding efforts in the best of times, we should be able to identify age-related problems that in a less favorable economic climate could be confused with the effects of recession.

Our first task was to find people who would be willing to talk to strangers on the telephone, candidly and at length, about their career reverses as well as their achievements. To reach potential respondents, we called about sixty organizations and agencies that serve older people in the Boston area in some way.

These included nonprofit career counseling programs for women and men of all ages, employment services for older job seekers, local offices of the state employment agency, officials in state and local government responsible for services to older citizens, for-profit employment and career agencies, and organizations of older people themselves.

We described the book we planned and our reasons for writing it, and asked for their assistance. In a follow-up letter we repeated the information and our request. We explained that we wanted to make contact with job seekers and job holders who had, at some time since they turned 50, experienced employment problems that they attributed to their age, emphasizing that we were looking for people who had not been fired "for cause," and who were not suffering from serious health or emotional problems. We wanted to interview men and women who had had at least five years of full-time paid employment in managerial, professional or technical jobs since 1970.

We requested that agencies ask any of their clients who fit this description to call us, or give us permission to call them, so that both sides could decide whether to make an appointment for an in-depth interview.

To gain the cooperation of potential respondents, we guaranteed them anonymity: We agreed not to use their real names, and to withhold the identity of their employers, past or present, as well as of the agencies they consulted about their job loss or during their job search. (The only exceptions we have made to this are references to government agencies whose records are open to the public.)

It proved far less difficult than we had anticipated to find suitable people to interview. Almost all the resources we contacted either referred one or more of their clients to us, or suggested other organizations or people to whom we could turn.

With only two or three exceptions, those people we asked for interviews granted them and answered our questions fully, some adding significant information and ideas that had not occurred to us when we drew up our interviewing plan. Their willingness to participate, they often told us, sprang from a desire to publicize the problem and help others in the same situation. Several people also referred us to others they knew who had had comparable experiences.

As we have explained in the introduction, we were already aware that considerably more mid-level men than women were coming forward with reports of lost jobs and difficulties in finding new employment. This proved true of the people we interviewed in the first weeks of our search. We therefore made a special effort to reach women by contacting women's organizations and several career programs for women at local colleges and universities. The final ratio of men to women in our sample was about 60:40, roughly the same as the division in the older work force as a whole.

We realized that pervasive racial discrimination prevented blacks of the pre–World War II generation from rising to mid-level professional or managerial jobs, but we made an effort to locate those who had in order to find out how age discrimination was affecting that small population.

With the aid of agencies and organizations serving the black community, we did find and interview a handful of minority men and women who were concerned about age-related job problems. As a black civil rights lawyer told us, "The older minority worker is still experiencing the old discrimination, and that is where their consciousness is. They haven't yet moved to that other plateau that says they are experiencing age discrimination."

In all, we interviewed about 125 people. In most cases the interviews were conducted in one session lasting from forty-five minutes to an hour or more. In some instances we held several conversations over a period of months. In others, we made a final follow-up call just before we began to write. A few interviews were discarded because the subjects had not engaged in a serious job search. We have included a few people not from Massachusetts. We had asked the help of agencies in New York and Washington at the beginning of our search, when we were not sure we would find sufficient willing interviewees closer to home.

Our sample is not a representative cross section of older workers, nor is it a random sample. It is "self-selected" in the sense that our interviewees identified themselves as older workers with age-related employment problems and actively chose to participate in our project. We hoped that by talking to a substantial number, we would be able to identify some typical patterns of age bias at work. We think we have.

More than half of the people we interviewed had a BA or BS degree. Some of the men had gone to college at night, after work; only a minority had gone to Ivy

League schools or obtained an advanced degree. As might be expected, a higher proportion of men than women had enrolled in nondegree, career-related courses. Women who had not gone to college were likely to have attended secretarial school or a junior college. Several were upgrading their skills at the time we interviewed them.

As for their occupations, few were top executives or highly paid professionals. The men had worked in middle level management or supervision, engineering, financial services, programming, purchasing, or sales. The women had been executive secretaries in office management and administration, bookkeeping, teaching, publishing, social work or healthcare, with a sprinkling in higher managerial positions requiring technical expertise.

The financial status of our male respondents was more precarious than we had expected. Many were still in their early or mid-50s and therefore not eligible for social security or pensions when they lost their jobs. Some had been given early, reduced pensions or other termination benefits. Most had received neither. Unemployment insurance helped while it lasted, but many were having trouble maintaining modest middle-class living standards.

The salaries they had earned in their last long-term jobs were correspondingly unimpressive, although they were well above the national average for their sex, as one would expect in a group with a high level of education and skills. More than half the men had earned between $30,000 and $40,000, about one-third less than $30,000, and only a handful $50,000 or more. Working full time had enabled them to pay off mortgages, send children to college, and complete installments on the car, but they had not been able to accumulate substantial cash reserves. Some still had children to support. A few had had to sell their homes, and others had to accept help from relatives. As might be expected, the women received substantially less than the men.

Almost three-quarters of the women had earned between $11,000 and $28,000 in their last full-time job or, if still employed, were in that salary bracket. Thirty-five thousand dollars was a high salary, and only three women earned in the $40,000–$50,000 range.

In addition to the earnings gap, the position of the men and women in our sample differed in another important respect. Four out of five of the men we interviewed were living with their spouses who, in many cases, were employed at least part time. Their contribution made it possible for the family to meet basic expenses and, sometimes, allowed the man to accept a low-paying job or hold out until the right job came along.

Three quarters of our women were divorced, separated, widowed, or had never married—a figure much higher than the national average for women of their age. We believe that women living alone are overrepresented in our interview population because they are the (growing) group most in need of securing their economic future entirely, or almost entirely, by their own efforts. They are, therefore, most aware of age discrimination and most devastated by it.

Our subjects were overwhelmingly self-made men and women, with no silver spoons in their background, or powerful sponsors to smooth their passage through the work world. Until recently they had been proud to have attained what their generation had been taught to strive for, a firm footing in the middle class.

2 | No-Fault Job Losers

Keep your nose to the grindstone. Do your job well. Be loyal to your company. By following this all-American work ethic, you would be assured of a long and healthy career. This had worked well for the men and many of the women we interviewed. They had never been unemployed for more than a few days since they took their first job. They had won regular raises and promotions, and had been looking forward to more of the same.

Those women who had entered the labor market after raising a family had not enjoyed such uninterrupted progress. Many, especially those who returned to paid employment after age 40, had had trouble locating good positions. Eventually, however, they had found jobs with their faith in the work ethic undamaged.

What had derailed these people from their career tracks at age 50 or, in the case of some women, even younger? Except for a few men who left their jobs for what they had thought were better opportunities, the blow was delivered by powerful external forces.

Age had played no part in the job losses for at least half the people we talked to, although it was the major obstacle to career recovery for almost everyone. Rather, unemployment was caused by the economic upheavals of the 1970s and 1980s that threw millions of men and women, young and old, out of work. Companies had closed plants, applied massive cutbacks, or gone out of business. Many saw their jobs disappear through mergers, buyouts, takeovers and other financial maneuvers, which may have been profitable for the principals but rendered the work ethic meaningless.

This chapter focusses on those cases of job loss where age did play a part. Events took a very different course for men than they did for women. Age was most clearly a factor in the cases of men who were employed by large companies that engaged in the cost-cutting early retirement plans referred to in the introductory chapter.

Long-term professional and managerial employees are natural targets. Their salaries are higher than those of more recently hired personnel at the same level because they have years of raises behind them. They are also closer to receiving maximum payoffs in retirement benefits. They are not covered by union or individual employment contracts that provide seniority rights. Letting them go is the easiest, quickest, and least risky economy measure.

Women of the same generation have rarely risen to those levels in large companies. They started and remained on nonprofessional tracks. Older women in mid-level jobs are more likely to be found in nonprofit organizations and smaller companies, and they often receive no special benefits when their jobs collapse.

Although employees over 50 are the ones affected by "exit incentive" programs, employers deny that age discrimination is involved. They explain their efforts to eliminate these middle-aged mid-level people as necessary restructuring measures to protect and improve the bottom line. Sometimes older workers are replaced by younger, lower priced, colleagues. Sometimes their expertise has been made obsolete by technology, allowing the remaining tasks to be assigned to lower level personnel, or new hires, or parcelled out to contract workers who cost less because they receive no benefits.

In order to show that the company is not singling out older people and that no one is being hurt, the severance is described as voluntary. The centerpiece of these incentive packages, offered to everyone in the category chosen for slimming, is usually an attractive pension proposal: Benefits will be paid beginning immediately to retirees who have not yet reached eligible age, although at a reduced rate. Other inducements may include a cash payment based on length of service and continued health plan coverage. The "window" in which the offer must be accepted is usually short, two or three months.

Good Fortune, Cut Rate

Acceptance rates are high. Some takers are reported to have been overjoyed at the chance to stop working and get paid for the privilege. The mid-level workers we talked to said yes because they were afraid to say no. They believed that job loss was inevitable, with lower or perhaps no benefits if they didn't jump at the offer before it expired.

Adrian N. was one of the reluctant takers when he accepted his employer's offer: eighteen months' salary plus early, reduced pension. He was 54, making $25,000, and had been working for the same large insurance firm for twenty-five years, first in sales and then in programming.

> They were aiming at everyone over 50 with ten or more years' service. They didn't make you retire but

they sure pushed you out. They had been giving me easier and easier work, and I no longer liked my job. It was a good offer, and I was sure I could get a better position.

Eventually he did find a better job, but it took nearly a year. The intervening months were full of shocks.

At first I enjoyed myself, Then I began looking for a programmer's job. I answered ads, went to agencies that specialize in those positions. It got me nowhere. I became very discouraged and depressed, began to lose confidence in myself, and finally I got lazy and stopped looking.

He became so despondent that he sought the help of a psychological counselor.

He got his break when his sister-in-law chanced to read an article about a retired businessman, working at one of the state employment service's job match centers, who specialized in helping older job seekers. Adrian went to see him. The service was elementary.

He told me to keep going through the job files. I saw something in New Bedford, and I went down. It paid much less than I had been earning, but I was interested. They weren't.

"Keep going through the job files," he said. Finally I came across a programming job for a language I knew but hadn't worked in, in years. My advisor told me to ask for an interview anyway. When I went there, a younger man was waiting for an interview too. They took me because he was asking twice as much money.

Adrian likes this new job better than his old one:

The work is more challenging, and I'm treated like everybody else instead of being given simple-minded tasks.

He has also had the satisfaction of being wooed by people who once cold-shouldered him.

I've had several phone calls recently from agencies that had nothing for me when I went to them. Now that the economy is good, they're trying to get me interested in jobs. One called this weekend saying they could get me a lot more money than I'm making. I may call him back.

The Perils/Profits of Resistance

Stephen M., a $68,000-a-year research chemist in senior management, dealt with his employer's early retirement offer quite differently. He discovered how ruthless companies can be towards employees who try to stay put. He also found that resistance can pay off.

I was a research fellow in charge of a group engaged in transforming research into products. This is a high-level job; only 200 people out of 16,000 in the company were in this senior grade. In 1981 I was trying to transfer to a pure research group and had been told by the head of that department that he would be happy to have me. As of November, everything was clear.

In December the company's so-called voluntary retirement plan was announced, and I was told that there was no longer any room for me in my present job, that the "head count" had to be reduced. I was also told that my transfer to Research had not been approved. I was 61, and I'd never thought of retiring. I'm not a person who goes in for hobbies; I depend on my work. The deadline for accepting the retirement package was February fifteenth, but as of the middle of January I got a 4 percent merit raise, so I felt reassured.

Then on February second my boss called me in just

at quitting time and gave me my performance evaluation. It was unsatisfactory. I had gone from excellent to unsatisfactory without any warning. Everything collapsed. The whole world turned upside down. There were no truths any more.

No one else in the company wanted me, I knew, because I had started exploring alternatives before I realized what was happening. I tried to make an appointment to see the senior vice president. Although I had always had access to him, he was suddenly too busy to see me. When I said I wanted to discuss my performance review, I was given an appointment six weeks in the future. He told me he had no reason to question the opinion of my boss, yet he had known my work longer than my boss had. He had the final say.

I knew that the purpose of the voluntary retirement plan was to get rid of the highest paid people and replace them with others at lower salaries, because this had been stated openly at a meeting of senior management which I attended. Most of the people there were going to implement the policy; I just turned out to be a victim.

At that meeting the vice president called the program a big opportunity, and he described how much pressure should be used and on whom. He said that normal layoffs would mean getting rid of younger people with lower seniority and lower pay, and that bigger numbers would have to go, thus threatening "the future of the company."

Not everyone accepted voluntary retirement, but my boss told me that in two months there would be actual firings and that my position would be abolished. There was no choice for me but to accept. I got one month's pay for each of my sixteen years of service.

Stephen M. was convinced that he had been forced to take retirement as the only alternative to termination, that his work became unsatisfactory only after his decision to reject the retirement package became known, and that his employer's treatment of him violated the Age Discrimination in Employment Act.

Stephen took a job as a $25,000 research assistant in the pharmaceutical department of a hospital, "back at what I was doing 40 years ago," as he put it. Meanwhile, his lawyer filed suit in federal court. After five years, the firm finally agreed to a six-figure settlement out of court, just before the case was scheduled to come to trial. We discuss the legal aspects of his case in Chapter Five.

Bennett E. managed to survive an additional two years in his $23,000 accounting job after his employer, a major Boston bank, tried to get him and other middle-level officers to retire early. He finally lost the battle at age 57, when the bank merged his department with two others, and found no place for him in the new department or anywhere else. The bank gave him one month's severance pay, a reduced pension, and continued membership in the health plan. He had worked there for fourteen years.

His troubles had begun when a new chief executive officer took over.

> He announced that he was going to make big profits. They started chopping off officers in their 50s and 60s because they didn't want to pay full pensions, and they put so much pressure on people that they left of their own accord. There were thirty to forty [people] in my department and they cut it down to six. I couldn't afford to leave, so they stopped giving me raises and started giving me poor evaluations.

As in the case of Adrian N., Bennett's job loss turned out to be advantageous in the end. Bennett got the first position he applied for, as an accountant to a nonprofit agency.

There's much less pressure and much more variety. I'd been having trouble with my heart, and now my doctor says I'm in the best shape in years. My salary is in the high teens. With my pension, I'm making $40–$50 a week more than I made at the bank.

Crimes and Punishments

Many of our respondents received little or nothing to soften the blow. Demotion with a $10,000 pay cut was the best alternative to dismissal Donald C. could wrangle from his employer, a large department store. He had joined the company ten years earlier, at age 47, and had worked his way up to a $27,000 job in operations management.

> I was 56, and I had just returned from vacation when the boss called me in and said, in effect, we're firing you; you're a lousy operator. I said, that's funny. A year ago you gave me a $3,000 raise and told me what a great job I was doing, and no one has told me anything different in between. They said, all right we'll make you a department manager. I had two kids in college at the time and I figured I'd better stay where I had some income. I tried to get hold of the personnel manager, but it was brought home to me that I'd be fired on the spot if I tried anything like that.

Donald was part of an extensive cost-cutting exercise.

> I could go on for a couple of hours about the other people who got let go before or after, because they pretty close to cleaned all the older people out. They'd take a merchandising manager and say either get out, or take a buying job. One merchandising manager I know is managing the warehouse sales now, a lower grade job. There was a senior vice president who they

couldn't really get to take a low enough job. They sent him down to the distribution center, hoping that would force him to leave.

A friend of mine in merchandising, who was fired about the same time I was threatened, had an interesting experience. When they told him what was going on he was shocked, but not so shocked that he didn't go immediately to personnel and make photocopies of his performance reviews. Some time after this he discovered that they had altered his records, but he had the original version! He hired a lawyer, and two years later they settled out of court. I wish I'd been smart enough to do that.

How did I feel? Angry at times, but I tried to realize that you shouldn't ruin yourself being upset with what's happened to you. It helped that you had so much company out there. It isn't like they said, Don, we're going to do a job on you. Sure they did, but they were doing it to hundreds of people at the same time.

Donald left the company after eighteen months in his low-level job, taking nothing with him but the dollars he had invested in the profit-sharing plan. His subsequent employment experiences and modest career comeback are described in Chapter Eight.

Conrad A. was dismissed overnight, with no warning and two weeks' pay after ten years with the company. He was a technical photographer with an engineering firm, earning $22,000, and was just 50 years old. The company had always relied on government contracts. Reductions in personnel often took place after contracts ended, "but never at my level," Conrad said. "I was shocked."

He believes his age caught up with him.

All my benefits were paid up. From then on, the company was supposed to pay everything. I was the highest paid in my group, the oldest, and also the only black.

Conrad immediately got job offers, but they were with photography labs, "all a step back for me." He decided to free-lance and now supplements his photography with two part-time jobs, one on a research project, the other managing a restaurant on the owner's day off. The combined income from all three sources is less than he had been earning in his last full-time job.

Reading Between the Lines

Age played a part, perhaps a major part, in the cost-trimming that put older women out of work. Its role was less clear cut, however, than in the case of men who worked for larger firms. The women, as a rule, worked in small firms and were rarely affected by mass reductions in mid-level personnel over 50. Instead, they were picked off individually.

Social service agencies showed no more consideration than the for-profit sector. Winnifred V. had worked for twenty-seven years for a small nonprofit agency aiding blind children when she was terminated at age 51 with two weeks' pay. The reason given in her written dismissal notice was lack of funding. She was earning $1,040 a month, and had no pension coverage and no health insurance.

> A month or so after I left I discovered that they had reopened my territory and hired a woman half my age to replace me. When I went to collect unemployment benefits I could not find my termination letter. Much to my shock, I learned I was ineligible for benefits because my former employer insisted that I had been fired for misconduct. He claimed he had never mentioned lack of funds.
>
> I probably should have taken the whole thing to court, but I was too crushed to do so at the time. About three years ago I did receive a very complimentary

letter from the agency's new director, who had known me and worked with me for years. The director who did me in was gone.

After being terminated I was really panicked and devastated. I stumbled along with some temporary jobs, some clerical nothing-jobs, brief self-employment and used up my savings. I was an expert in the field of blind children's development, and I could not get a job that would use those skills.

It took me some years to gain the confidence to apply for civil service jobs, but I passed the tests with high scores. At age 54 I started all over. I am a county welfare worker, a job that requires only a high school degree. At 59 I'm on a promotional waiting list; it will be years before I get the chance to use my full education and training, but at least I'm on the way.

Flora D., a full-charge bookkeeper with thirty years of experience, was marked for dismissal at age 55, less than a year after she started working for a small appliances firm.

Things went wrong from the very beginning. A few weeks after Flora started, the comptroller who had hired her was fired.

She was pregnant. Of course they didn't say that was the reason, but it was obvious.

While I was there, two women in the sales department were let go. One was my age, one a little younger, and they were both replaced by younger women. One day the vice president came in and he said, in a laughing way, "Come on, let's get some people here under 40." I was there and a woman of about 45 and someone about 39. It was supposed to be some kind of a joke.

Then they put an ad in the paper for my job. They had done the same thing with another older woman. They kept her on until they hired someone younger and cheaper, and then they told her on Friday not to come on Monday. I asked the comptroller point blank whether the job was my job or for the helper they had talked about getting me.

He hemmed and hawed and finally said it was my job, that it was a matter of economics. They had no criticism of my work. I had just gotten the raise I was promised from the start, and was making $9.20 an hour.

Flora stayed on a few weeks to train the new recruit, a woman in her 30s. "After a while I started to feel like a lame-duck president and I just wanted to get out."

When Elsa G. lost her public relations job with a national health care firm she didn't believe their explanation that the company was reducing its work force. She was convinced that age was the real reason and that her younger colleagues were accomplices. She was 52 and had always held jobs combining educational and organizational responsibilities.

I had been there for four years and was earning in the upper teens. For the first three-and-a-half years I went out to schools and colleges to recruit people for health-care education. Then I was called to another state to do training. It was a promotion, and I really thought I was on an upward track.

Trouble started, she thinks, when her boss had her demonstrate her training techniques to a group of younger colleagues.

That was the kiss of death. When you talk to strangers it doesn't matter how old you are. In fact, age is an asset because they think you really must know something. But with 30-year-old coworkers, it's another matter.

My boss probably put me forward as someone really fabulous, and I think they reacted with she's not so great, who does she think she is? They want to be the ones doing it. Where money is involved, they are out for themselves. They don't want to see the money go to an older person. They're like kids with their parents: Hey, you don't need the money, I do.

Soon after this session, personnel began asking Elsa her age for the first time in the four years she had worked there.

I had never put it on the forms, but they kept pressing me, saying they needed it for insurance. I finally gave in. I think the last straw was that I was out for two weeks with back pains from lifting one of their projectors. I had never missed a day's work until then. When you're over 50 and get sick, the myth is that you're going to be out a lot because you're menopausal.

A month or so later, as Elsa G. describes it, she was

phased out. Times are tough, they said. We're revamping, reducing the work force. I got a couple of weeks' salary, lost my years towards pension and my medical benefits.

The Unkindest Cut

On St. Patrick's Day, 1986, "a load of bricks fell on me," Madeleine J. told us.

It was the day I returned from the first real break I had taken from work for years, a trip to India. "Madge, dear friend," said my boss and patron who had given me my first opportunity at the firm, "I'm afraid we'll have to let you go."

Madeleine was one of the highest paid women we interviewed. She was earning $34,000 as public relations director for the design firm where she had been employed for seven years. Her tragedy had an ironic twist.

> The day I left for India, my boss and dear friend had called me in to say they would have to let my assistant go because of cost cutting. She's 31. I protested passionately, built her up, got him to promise to wait until I returned before he did anything. When I came back the script had changed; I was leaving, she was staying.
> I'll never know what happened while I was away. She may have sensed that something was in the works and shone in my absence, champing at the bit to run the show. The firm had been financially pressed for the last couple of years, with layoffs and early retirement for older staff. The place was mismanaged, going downhill.
> I asked my boss if my self-effacing remarks had anything to do with the change of scenario. He said "No, economic reorganization." Franny, my assistant, would be answering to the marketing manager. He was a man of her age and I knew he didn't like me. "While you were away," my boss said, "Fran proved that she could fill your shoes."

Madeleine negotiated an above average consolation: three months' pay, an extra year's service credit toward her pension, and the privilege of using her office to maintain the fiction that she was still working while she searched for a job.

> Everyone in the firm offered help and sympathy. After the first six weeks I realized that the help I needed was offered only by professionals. I saw a career counselor. She helped me realize how depressed I was and that I needed therapy.

Another career counselor gave very different advice.

The whole focus was to document everything so that I could file an age discrimination suit. This was also mentioned to me by older people the firm had sacked. But I'm not a fighter, and besides if you want another job, doing something like that can blackball you.

Better Safe Than Sorry

The second counselor's advice to Madeleine was right, we believe. But it was given at the wrong time, in the wrong way. People age 40 and over should document their employers' actions and words from the time the first hint of job loss surfaces until the last day at work, whether or not they think age discrimination is involved or intend to take any legal action. Their perception of age discrimination and its role in their job loss is almost certain to sharpen when they try to find another position.

The value of keeping a "diary of dismissal" is hard to get across to someone who has not thought about age and employment. Most of our interviewees were in this category when their job losses took place. Some were sure they would have no trouble finding other jobs because they had so many years of experience, not realizing that those years would be a liability, not an asset. Others, like Madeleine, were stunned by their misfortune at first, then felt severely wounded at being cast aside and worried about their career futures.

Madeline was one of very few who sought career counseling during this period. The second counselor who saw her apparently did not respond to her need for reassurance and support for her efforts to plan how and where to look for a job. Instead, the counselor assumed that Madeleine was aware of age discrimination and in condition to fight the dismissal.

Most of the men and women we talked to became aware of age bias gradually during months of job searching. Only then did they suspect that age discrimination was involved in their dismissal. Either it was too late to do anything about it because the deadline for filing complaints had passed, or the details of who said or did what and when had blurred over time. As they put it, "There was no evidence."

Even if dismissal diaries are not used to provide such evidence to antidiscrimination agencies or private attorneys, they are helpful defensive weapons. Some interviewees had trouble obtaining unemployment benefits because employers contested their applications, claiming they were fired for cause. In Chapter Ten, we recommend keeping or making copies of all written statements from employers pertaining to the employee's job performance and job termination, but employers do not put everything, sometimes even anything, in writing. Maintaining a detailed record of their deeds and oral statements is additional insurance for obtaining unemployment benefits and can also counteract a bad reference or its equivalent, refusal to provide any reference at all.

Describing the termination ordeal on paper every day may be painful. But it ventilates feelings and dilutes and diminishes stress. It can also clarify problems and make them easier to bear. The record can also be a source of comfort by offering proof to the job loser and anyone he or she talks to about dismissal that the employer, not the victim, has performed poorly.

And job losers should talk to sympathetic, experienced listeners about what's happening to them, while it's happening. Spouses and other family members are often too distressed themselves to respond objectively. A competent therapist is one option to consider. The cost of several sessions may be covered by the employee's health insurance. Many programs include mental health services, stipulating the qualifications for professionals who are eligible for payment.

Several of the men we interviewed sought professional help for the first time in their lives months after leaving work. Post-job-loss depression had crippled them, and their doctors or spouses had urged them to get help. Their health benefits were still in effect because their employers had allowed them to pay the premiums in order to stay in the companys' plans. Professional counseling, they reported, rebuilt their confidence and stamina.

If talking to a therapist is not possible or desirable, job losers should talk to a friend, their doctors or ministers, someone whose judgment they respect. That's what people do when someone near and dear dies. Job loss at middle age is less tragic, but it is traumatic and does cause real grief. Weathering it alone can prolong suffering and impede recovery.

Middle-aged Expendables

The job-loss stories presented here are not worst-case scenarios. Other interviewees had similar experiences when companies sought to solve their financial problems at the expense of mid-level personnel. Large corporations, small businesses, and nonprofit agencies all behaved with equal disregard for middle-aged employees' long service and their emotional investment in their jobs.

Losing a job is a blow whatever the reason and however the dismissal is handled. Respectful treatment can limit ego damage, and termination benefits can compensate for some of the pain. Only a few of our respondents, usually men, received such benefits; and the severance process was far from humane. Executives of companies whose names are household words humiliated older men who had served the firms well for years by imposing demotions or poor performance ratings to get them to leave quickly and quietly. Colleagues and bosses added insult to injury by showing contempt and hostility toward older women.

If the job loss had been followed immediately by a job find, the price paid by older workers for employer savings would have been low. As the next chapters on their job searches reveal, the quests were long and rarely ended in complete success. New employers were reluctant to hire them for the same reasons that the previous employers had fired them: Age had made them expendable.

3 | JOB-HUNTING: TRAILS AND TRIALS

The first objective in every job search is getting an interview with a favorably disposed employer or company representative. The traditional methods are answering ads, writing cold to companies in your field, and registering with employment agencies. Sounds obvious, but as we will see in this chapter, age barriers block the way. It takes more than conventional methods to hurdle them.

> If we were working now we'd be the grand old men of the company, the company sages. Because we're not employed, people think, there must be something wrong with you, you ought to be vice president at your age.

So spoke Arthur K., 57, a chemist with thirty-two years of experience. He had forfeited his $40,000 job in industrial research and development three years earlier as the loser in an "internal company war." Since then, he has been unemployed, except for a seven-month stint that he describes as a mistake.

He was talking to us about middle management and professional men like himself, who lost jobs when they were in their mid-50s. But he put his finger on a universal truth: The older job hunter carries an invisible stigma along with the visible grey hairs.

To the public in general, and even to older people who aren't job hunting, the unemployed older worker evokes stereotyped reactions: If they had been any good to begin with they wouldn't be out of a job. They must be slowing down, out of date. Or, if it has been established that the older worker is the victim of a mass layoff or merger, they aren't looking hard enough; don't know how to present themselves (they oversell, undersell); or are too fussy. They want too much money, or they won't consider changing fields. They won't or can't develop new skills. Maybe they're unwilling to relocate.

Of course it is not true that an older worker is always better qualified than the younger candidate who gets the position, or that older people never muff an interview. Some do have a chip on their shoulder or come across as downbeat because they are discouraged and are winding down their search. Some try to hold out for their old pay; a few even get it. And of course you can always present yourself better.

The question is, Does reaching age 50 stamp men and women with indelible qualities that make them less desirable workers than younger people? The case histories we have collected show that there is no "over 50" pattern of behavior to justify employers' attitude towards them.

Age is not central to the older worker's self-image, at least not at first. It often takes the mature job hunter months to realize why answers to ads and sending out resumes bring no replies, why interviews never produce offers.

Everyone over 40 has experienced the feeling of being a young spirit captive in an aging body: "I know

I'm 61, but I'm really 48." "I'm only 25 in my head. I'm at my peak." If our interviewees did not feel that way, they could not have displayed the tenacity that characterizes them as a group—out there still pounding the pavements or the typewriter, smiling their way through interviews, adjusting their sights to jobs they once would not have considered or, in a few cases, achieving a comeback.

When they lost or left their jobs, it had never occurred to most that they would have serious trouble finding others. The majority had not been through the job-hunting ordeal since they found their first positions, although this was less true for the women than the men.

Typically, the men had uninterrupted employment histories. When they had changed jobs it was because they had relocated or been offered better positions before they left their old ones. "I never had to look before," said one. "I could always choose what I wanted." By the time we got to know them, they had been exposed to a heavy dose of reality. It is through their experiences that we were able to see the obstacles barring employment of older professionals and managers in today's job market.

Working the Want Ads

Employers know the law. They do not any longer mention age in their ads. But they have other ways of getting the message across. The ad that begins "Young, aggressive company" seeks "bright, energetic" office manager, purchasing agent, engineer or secretary is sending a clear signal. Many companies, particularly in high technology, specify years of experience as a way of indicating what they want. It's usually two–three or three–five years, sometimes as many as ten–fifteen for executive posts. The implication is that no one with a twenty-five-year employment record need apply.

Having learned how to read selectively, "My day is built around the newspaper," an engineer told us. He checks off every ad that looks at all promising and sends out one of several resumes that he has written with the aid of a job counselor, attaching an individually crafted cover letter. He details only the last fifteen to twenty years of his work experience, or lists the companies he has worked for without dates, and summarizes his qualifications and achievements. Of course he does not mention his age or the dates of his academic degrees. Nevertheless, he rarely gets a reply. "The more you've done, the more you give yourself away."

That is a general observation. Answers to ads bring few responses, and even fewer invitations to interviews. When a meeting does take place, "It's impossible to prove anything," but often it seems clear to the interviewee that the person across the desk had been expecting someone younger.

"I got some interviews," a former packaging manager in the food industry told us. "My problem was that they'd get my resume and it looked good. Let's talk to this guy, they'd decide. Then they'd see me come in the door and realize my age. They'd be nice, then send a letter later that they'd found someone more suited."

Not all were so nice. A secretary recalls: "I began to notice that I was not being given a test in many companies where it was customary to do so. The interviews lasted a noticeably brief time. In one instance I had barely sat down when the interviewer got up and left, saying something important had come up and he could not continue, but would call me to reschedule. I never heard from him again."

According to a man with recent sales and management experience in the computer industry, "You can tell. Within the first few minutes after they see you, they start talking in generalities. They don't describe the specifics of the job. I've interviewed lots of people for jobs myself. When you see someone and you know you don't want them, you find it difficult to cut the conversation off so you keep it going nowhere."

Fee-charging Agencies

In spite of discouragement, some older applicants did secure jobs through the Help Wanted ads. Several even found positions they liked very much. Almost no one, on the other hand, had kind words for the employment agencies that find full-time jobs for applicants for a fee paid by the hiring firm. Older workers feel that they are given the brush off. Agency personnel, usually young, are not interested in figuring out how an older person with manifold experience could fit their job orders.

Actually these agencies are being realistic. They are not in the do-good business, and they are not paid to be innovative. They know what their employer-clients want. They want young people who will come in at the lower salaried echelons of a job category and grow with the job. They want recently tooled technicians and professionals, not old hands. As evidence, the personnel director of a large private New York City hospital cited his own daily experience: "When I present two or three people, they inevitably take the youngest, regardless of qualifications."

A former manager of systems development, out of work at 55, reports: "I worked for a few months with a friend who was starting an employment agency, but I couldn't stand it. We'd get job requisitions from well-known high tech companies saying no one over 40. You know how that goes. You take the most saleable candidate and push them. To hell with the others."

Free Agencies

Another class of agencies, the state-run employment service and the nonprofit agencies that sponsor publicly supported job-finding programs, serve older job seekers and employers free of charge. Nonprofit agencies are usually required by their government grants to gear their services to low-income older workers.

In Massachusetts, twenty-eight of these nonprofit agencies are part of a network known as ABLE, which began in the Boston area in 1983. Like the other ABLE networks in California, New York, and other states, the Massachusetts organization is modeled on Operation ABLE of Chicago, which was established in 1977 to focus on the employment problems of people over 55. ABLE hears from job seekers and from employers with openings, and generally refers callers to affiliated agencies for help. It also sponsors several programs that serve both groups directly. Its work is financed by government grants, with some support from corporations, foundations, and individuals.

Most clients who apply to these agencies are referred to openings that pay less than $6.00 an hour, many of them part time. Recently, the number of skilled and experienced older applicants has increased sharply. Some, who have been out of work for several years, meet federal low-income standards. Whether they do or not, these men and women want to get back into well-paying, responsible full-time jobs.

Some nonprofit employment agencies have tried to help, but this calls for a qualitatively different approach from that used in placing older people in entry-level jobs. Above all, it means generating commitments from the business community to hire qualified older people in mid-level openings.

At present, these agencies are strong on workshops

and advice, but lack access to mid-level openings and the high-level executives who make décisions about them. In 1986 more than 40% of applicants to the Boston ABLE network were professional, technical, or managerial workers. Only 16% of the jobs listed with ABLE were in this category.

"Very nice people but the help they give is mostly mental," a merchandising manager commented politely. "All the suggestions were things I had already been doing," a former executive secretary told us. "I wanted some idea of what their contacts had been, what companies might be interested in me."

The most disappointing experience was recorded by a 58-year-old senior administrator, unemployed for two years, who applied for help to a private nonprofit agency on the strength of a newspaper report about its "new thrust" in the direction of mid-level job seekers.

Over a three-month period he contacted them regularly. He was given only three names of companies to visit, on the understanding that his resume had been sent ahead and that they were receptive. Only one lead produced an actual job interview. A second resulted in a courtesy interview, but no job was available. In the third instance, a personnel officer had supposedly been impressed with his resume and promised to circulate it. When he called, however, the officer in question had no recollection of the resume or the promise, and had no opening that matched the applicant's qualifications.

Understandably, this middle-management candidate felt that, good intentions aside, the agency's new thrust exceeded its grasp, and that the staff did not have the capacity or the contacts to handle placements at the administrative or professional level. He thought that having his resume circulated under these conditions might do him more harm than good. So he withdrew as an agency client.

Cultivating Service Agencies

Suggestions for public and nonprofit agencies on ways and means to produce more effective assistance for older job seekers appear in Chapter 10. Older job seekers themselves can strengthen agency output by becoming more assertive clients. Our interviewees, and their generation, are not accustomed to dealing with social workers and others in the helping professions. And self-advocacy and confrontational tactics are not their style. When agencies did not provide the help they needed, they did not press persistently for better service. They stopped using the agency.

The middle manager just described did try to get a better deal by writing to the acting director of the agency. But his letters circled around the problem, and he gave up too soon. If he had continued for several months to press the staff politely but firmly and directly for referrals to middle-level openings, they might have delivered on their publicly stated promises.

Older people are reluctant to criticize agencies. They seem to think that the staff are doing them a favor. That is not so, of course. The nonprofit agencies are financed directly or indirectly by taxpayers. Their responsibility is to provide assistance, and they should be held accountable when they fall short.

Campaigning for attention from a service provider is not easy when job loss and fruitless job search have shaken self-confidence. But unless older clients are more assertive, agencies are apt to neglect their needs and deal with less prickly tasks. It is very difficult to get employers to consider older people for decent jobs. Agencies rarely state that fact publicly. So even if persistent pressure does not result in better service for the individual, it can make the agency face up to the problem.

Job Fairs

Job fairs are designed to provide an easy entree to job interviews. They are shopping malls for employers and job hunters. The latter pay nothing to attend. At fairs run as commercial ventures, pirating is in the wind. Participating firms pay a hefty sum to set up a booth or table to attract hard-to-get young computer professionals, nurses, engineers, and other technical specialists. Companies also buy into fairs to lure secretaries, bookkeepers, word processors and other hard-to-find clericals. These people are likely already to have jobs, and the point is to offer them inducements to change.

"I was at a job fair and I met with two corporation representatives," a construction engineer, age 55, reported.

> One, from an electronics type company, told me: First of all you're too old, forget it. As far as we're concerned, any engineer over 35 is burned out and useless.
>
> I said, you gotta be kidding. He said, oh no, we've found that out from experience. They get into a set pattern, they're not open to new ideas. Everything changes so radically and so quickly, unless you can absorb all these new ideas today and forget them tomorrow, you're no use to us.

When the engineer happened to meet this same man again in other circumstances, the company representative said,

> Oh, I remember you. What I told you the other day, you know that really is company policy, and it's the worst policy going. What happens is that when we hire these young kids out of school and we train them to where

we want them, then they leave. So they're good for about two years. Whereas if we hire an older person the chance of their leaving is nil until they retire.

Why don't they change their policy? I don't know.

Job fairs specifically for older applicants are a recent development. They are sponsored by government or voluntary agencies, and employers pay a nominal registration fee only. Mid-level older workers attend in the hope of finding something in their line. We have never known them to succeed. Interviewees and other fair goers report that openings are no more than a step or two above entry level. Whatever their advance billing, such fairs are primarily an opportunity for firms to recruit office workers, sales clerks, and food service personnel.

Job fairs would not be entirely no-win events if older people protested and exposed unfair practices. The sponsors, especially government agencies and nonprofit agencies supported by government funds, might then review the job listings to be offered by employers at the fair and try harder to attract companies with mid-level opportunities.

When advance publicity states that a fair will have jobs "at all levels," or uses similar phrases, older people should ask recruiters for information about openings above entry- and semiskilled levels. They should ask for job title, salary range, and qualifications and write down the answers under name of company and recruiter. If positions are available, they can fill out applications, request interviews, and leave resumes.

If no or few mid-level openings are forthcoming, the job seeker should report this experience to the fair sponsor(s), with a short note stating that the publicity was misleading and requesting a response. The same information can be sent to the leading local newspaper, television news program, and radio talk show, with a cover letter stating that older job seekers, qualified and eager for mid-level work, came to the fair, misled by its publicity. The letter must be signed to be credible. But the signator can request that his or her identity be kept in confidence if the information is made public. The media may look into the problem or be on the look-out for other examples of false promises about work for older people. Any media coverage about the difficulties facing older job seekers is helpful. Public consciousness on the need for institutional reforms is very low. Raising it is essential.

Why should older people go to the trouble of making these efforts? How can it benefit them personally? Putting up with unfair come-ons means wasting hard-to-get public funds for career assistance to older people. Taking the initiative to document what is wrong takes very little time, carries very little risk, and can produce better opportunities for older, mid-level fair goers.

How did our older workers go about seeking jobs? Did they give up too easily, lack flexibility, and willingness to adapt? Were they obsolete? Why did things turn out the way they did?

No Matching What You Had

All the job counselors we talked to stressed that an unemployed older professional or manager must be prepared for a comedown in salary and responsibility. Luther H., formerly a sales executive and now himself a job counselor for a voluntary agency, simply tells clients what happened to him.

Luther believes his first "mistake" was in not checking the financial solidity of his new employer when he changed jobs in 1978 at the age of 58. He jumped at the chance to move back to New England. "I should have known there was something wrong for them to hire an old-timer like me." Within a year the company went bankrupt.

I did all the things we do in sales and marketing. I sent out 300 individually typed letters to 300 individuals in Dun and Bradstreet. I contacted executive search agencies, but I only heard from three. The others must have sensed that I was old, although I didn't realize that then. I got nibbles from a couple of companies that interviewed me on the telephone, and then they trailed off. I ran my own ads in trade papers. I bought a clipping service with all sales and marketing ads this side of the Mississippi. I contacted former employers and employees I'd helped.

A friend sent me to a private consultant who came up dry, but he passed my file along to a friend in a personnel job to check the references in case there was some bad news out there we didn't know about. Everything checked out great, but the shocker in the letter I'll never forget. His references are impeccable but his age is a cold shower. Eighteen months after I started looking I suddenly realized I was in deep trouble.

I needed money. I had kids, a son in college. I was spending my principal. I had to get something to do. I was up against a blank wall, reduced to a piece of junk. Not part of the human race.

Ready to take anything, he saw a job advertised by a nonprofit agency. The contact eventually led to counseling older workers like himself. Now 64, he has been at it for two years, enjoys the work, and considers himself lucky. He spends a great deal of time talking to employers and trying to break down prejudice against older applicants. "We're slowly building up a list of companies that are more receptive than others," is the cautious way he describes the results.

I've done fantastic things in my career in industry. Now I rap on a door, they see my face. Forget it. They think, Oh God, here comes my grandfather. I make 25% of what I used to make. Got rid of the house, the car. The wife went to work. The first thing I tell people who come to me, and it's a bombshell, you're not going back to the work you used to do at the money you used to get. Swallow the pill first.

Sense of Direction Needed

Alice E. is an example of someone who needs first-rate career counseling and help in developing networking skills. She has managerial skills but does not know how or where to put them to use. We apologized to her for phoning her on a Sunday morning, but she was glad to be disturbed. "I'm sitting here reading the want ads and feeling miserable," she told us.

Alice once owned her own beauty shop, later was hired as cosmetics buyer by a top New York department store, and finally worked for nine years recruiting and training cosmeticians for one of the country's largest beauty chains. The training program ended when the company was sold in 1984. She learned that other large beauty firms were phasing out their training programs as well. She quickly found a position in a decorator's show room through a friend. That business folded in 1985, leaving her unemployed for the first time in eighteen years.

After six months of unemployment, she took a customer service job with a small furniture service firm. She fed data into a computer, with constant interruptions to answer one of several telephones or to make coffee. This is unquestionably a setback for a woman of 58 who had been earning $35,000 plus expenses in 1984. Her employers know it, she believes, since they met her demand of $20,000 when she refused the offered $18,000. "It's awful," she says, "I've never felt like this, but it's a job."

Neither ads nor agencies work for her, she claims.

Either I'm overqualified or I'm underqualified. I look through the paper. They want cosmeticians, but I'm not a licensed cosmetician. I'm trained in electrolysis. They want manicurists. I could do that, but it doesn't pay enough. I've been to several employment agencies. When they see my background they think it's weird. They don't know what to do with me. I don't have office skills. But I'm very good at managing and organizing, at getting it all together, coordinating, improving. I would love to get into personnel, but they don't think I have the experience for it.

I'd be good in the travel business, but they want managers who have experience in that field. In real estate you work on commission and that's risky. If I had a year I could probably go to school and learn something else. I'd like that, and I learn very quickly. But I live alone, and I'm self-supporting.

I took this job because it pays more than unemployment; $180 a week doesn't cover anything and you get kind of scared. Living in this area you will have used up your savings. Besides, when you are collecting unemployment insurance you don't accomplish anything. You get up every morning and you look at the want ads and you get nauseous. The whole day is wasted because you haven't got the energy any more to do anything. You sit around and feel guilty.

I'm going to try to manage by getting a Saturday job to earn another $50. Rents are high. I think my apartment is going condo in about two years so then what do I do?

Many people find themselves in Alice's position, with good, nonspecific skills but concrete experience in a disappearing field. While willing to retool herself for a new career in which she could make use of her organizational abilities and her talent for handling people, she cannot afford to invest heavily in a future with uncertain prospects. She joined a support group and found it lifted her spirits. But it could not change what she has to offer an employer.

There are still things Alice can do. Her next step should be to call her nearest YM/WCA or community college and find out where low-cost career counseling is available. She could also ask about workshops or conferences on career possibilities in expanding fields. Short-term courses are available in business skills that are useful in a variety of jobs. At the very least, she should develop computer expertise. Her situation is difficult, but not hopeless.

Put-Downs

I'm a generalist, administrator, manager, program developer. I have a lot of experience. I have always worked. I'm keyed into the world of work. I've never married, and I am dependent on my income for my livelihood. For the last nine-and-a-half years I have been in health administration.

That's how Peggy O., 57, introduced herself to us. At the beginning of 1984 she resigned from a hospital job as director of community health education for a more challenging position in state government. After a little more than a year, her immediate superior resigned as did another senior woman administrator. Peggy was informed that the department would be reorganized and there was no place for her.

The climate was very youth oriented, and there was an institutional ethos which almost glowed in neon when they talked about it. It had to do with fiscal responsibility, sometimes to the detriment of human considerations. It was supposed to be a new development, and I think younger people were perceived as

being more "with it" while we older people were
bleeding hearts.

I didn't concentrate on my dismissal as being an
age-related issue because it was too stunning for me. I
had worked very hard under very difficult conditions,
and suddenly, kaboom!

Two experiences in the ensuing months of disappointing search stand out for her.

A friend suggested I go to see the director of a
nonprofit career service, simply to find out what information they had about places and people to talk to. I
met with a chill from the very beginning. The director,
a women in her 40s, had invited the placement
woman, who was my age or older, to attend.

I said that I had begun to realize that my age was a
factor even when I went on information interviews.
The placement woman said, that's ridiculous. Age is
not a factor unless you put it there. I said I don't
believe that's true. I think we live in a climate where
age has a lot of bad press and people have very strong,
mostly negative feelings about growing older.

She said, "that's just nonsense." It went on and on.
It was the most self-damaging meeting I've ever had.
People can deny their own experience all they want,
but I have a hard time when they start denying mine.

It had been extremely painful for me to to admit
that indeed my age had become a factor, hard because
I am in very good physical shape and I don't think I
necessarily represent people's negative image of an
older worker. I had had to realize that it doesn't really
matter what you are as an individual. You're tarred
with the same brush.

Peggy's other crushing memory was her experience
with a young man in a major insurance company who
was hiring an administrator for its employee health
plan. At the first interview, he told her that she was the

best candidate to date, but he was afraid they could not afford her. When she mentioned her price, he said: "Well, that is close to the top, but you certainly have the experience to justify it."

At a second meeting it was clear that she was still in the running. "I didn't feel from this younger man any of the kind of negative stuff you get, not at all. Yet he called me on the last day of the waiting period to tell me he had chosen someone else. He said, 'I want to explain that I felt it was because you were overqualified.'"

Now I do think that's a code word. There's no way to demonstrate it, but I believe that in the mix of the decision he found someone he felt less threatened by or more able to train. I think "overqualified" means that someone has made a decision and is looking for a kind of cover. It saves them from having to expose their own feelings and ask themselves, Why don't I want this person? Am I afraid of her? Is it like working with my mother?

After a while we believe all the things that are said about us as a class. And that is the most destructive thing of all, because then we begin to act the way people said we would act. If I just don't give in to this terror I sometimes feel, I think I will find an interesting next thing to do.

When we last spoke to Peggy, after six months of unemployment, she had been promised a job with a hospital personnel training program—if the program materialized. Like all her other jobs and near jobs, this contact came through a friend.

Luck or Leverage?

"Whatever happens, don't give up," are famous last works of job counselors everywhere. Rita N. is an example of what those words can mean.

At 42, Rita took a year off to recover from a series of misfortunes: her father's death, her husband's death, and the loss of her $45,000 job as marketing director with a big publishing firm in one of their periodical mass layoffs.

> Losing my job was devastating because it had been my identity. I had to look into myself and come to terms with it. But taking a break in my working life was a big mistake.

She felt that her age required her to lower her sights. When she did, she found employers were reluctant to hire someone with her experience in a lower level job. Finally she decided to take a temporary position and to continue the search, this time holding out for what she wanted.

> Basically I had no clerical skills. All I knew was inside my head, and people don't want that in a low-paying job.

Consequently, the temporary jobs she got were, to use her word, "bizarre." She managed the life of a twenty-eight-year-old millionaire, but she couldn't stand his drug habit. Then she was maid-of-all work for a public relations firm of seven people and two dogs. Meanwhile she continued the hunt.

After a year of routine search beginning in March 1985, Rita intensified her efforts.

> I put in nine hours a day for these people, I put in another eight for myself. I used to get up at four in the morning and type twenty to twenty-five cover letters to send out with my resumes, and then at night when I came home from work I would continue: Answers to ads and blind letters to publishing companies and

other companies, advertising agencies, corporations that had advertising and marketing departments, head hunters.

I remember walking to work one morning and the thought of suicide crossed my mind. I said no way. I knew I had to put forth superhuman effort.

I answered ads in Arizona, Washington, D.C., Maine. I sent out about 500 letters. I followed them up with second letters and with phone calls. I didn't care if I had to relocate as long as it was something well-paying. I took a course on career changing for executives. It wasn't helpful; it just gave me a feeling I was doing something.

In the end, which was ten months later, in January, 1986, she landed the job she wanted, with another publishing company.

It was a fluke. I suddenly remembered this head hunter I had known fifteen years ago. He had already talked to forty people. I saw him on a Thursday, I was interviewed on Monday, and I was hired on Wednesday.

It was just chance that I called him. It all boils down to being in the right place at the right time. All the other things are busywork unless you have direct contacts in the field that open the doors so you can walk right in.

Rita got the job through someone she knew. Like some other men and women we will meet in the next chapter, she saw being in the right place at the right time as nothing but pure luck.

Looking for a job is monotonous, wearing work. Chapter Ten prescribes several "tonics" that can stimulate new thinking and generate fresh energy during the search—career workshops, job-seeker support groups, information interviewing. But these and other infusions relate to job finding. A complete change in milieu is also recommended to avoid atrophying and burnout, the occupational hazards of single-minded pursuits.

Take a course or a training program that has nothing to do with job finding, per se, but can lead to expanded career possibilities. We suggest computer skills or sales/marketing techniques. Both are offered by many community colleges, adult education centers, and other low-fee sponsors. Investing a few hours a week and a few hundred dollars, at most, will develop skills that everyone needs to get along in today's work world, whatever their chosen field.

4 | WEAVING A SAFETY NET

Some of the job seekers we interviewed lowered age barriers to come closer to the job they wanted by creating a network of contacts. They learned that working with peers who are also seeking employment can enhance the process. A good outplacement agency takes it one step further by helping an older worker develop a new sense of direction.

Who You Know

Using personal contacts in your field and others to open doors to employment possibilities may sound like an obvious job-search technique. But when we asked the interviewees whether they called on former colleagues, business associates, neighbors, friends, relatives, or anyone else they knew for ideas and leads during their job quest, more often than not the answer was "No, it's my own problem, I was too proud, they knew what my situation was and didn't call me." Men, particularly, seem ashamed to admit that they need help, afraid of being seen as failures.

After repeated disappointments with conventional job-search methods, those men and women who tried it are convinced that help for older workers lies in systematic networking with professional and personal contacts. The job seeker must first find people who will treat him or her as an individual rather than as an older person. Such people are likely to give advice and suggest others to call. One contact leads to another, and that's how networks are spun.

Do It Yourself

Some job seekers networked on their own. Others joined support groups. A few were referred by employers to outplacement services that helped them initiate and strengthen the networking process.

Arthur K., the 57-year-old chemist quoted at the beginning of Chapter Three, is an example of a networking loner. He has a broad base in the industry, having worked in vacuum, power plant and both low and high temperature technologies, as well as glass consumer products. After two-and-a-half years of unproductive job searching, he decided to try his expertise in another field, environmental protection, by networking into it.

I'm convinced it's the only way to go. A fellow I met gave me some names and there are a number of other sources. I'm going down the list. It's an extremely complicated network, with cross-referencing and several names in the same organization.

It's also a slow process. You write a letter asking for a meeting, making plain that you're not looking for employment, just advice. You have to give time for the letter to arrive. You have to make a phone call, and the chances are you won't get through the first time. In my experience it takes not less than three weeks from the day you write until you meet the person, sometimes longer.

I've found that all the people I've contacted have talked to me. So far there are only two out of twenty-five or thirty I haven't been able to reach. I've met with all the others. They all say there should be a place for me; the question is where. So far it looks good, but only time will tell.

Networking is an acquired skill. Daniel A. and Barbara D. are typical job seekers in that they were not aware that they were neglecting their best resources. Both eventually found jobs through personal contacts, but by chance rather than design, and only after months lost in demoralizing encounters with personnel and other job interviewers.

Better Late than Never

Ten years ago Daniel A., now 63, was a successful bank treasurer with ambitions to open his own bank. He did so only to be caught between the low mortgage rates offered to borrowers in 1977 and the high interest rates paid to customers in 1979. Interest payments to the bank were at the old, low rate, while the interest the bank paid its customers was several points higher. The bank was forced to close for lack of reserves.

A spell as an accountant with a small firm ended when the venture went broke. Then came answering the ads in the *Wall Street Journal*, the trips to head hunters.

I had thirty-two years of banking experience, several as chief operating officer plus an accounting background. The talent scouts did nothing for me.

I was advised to tone down my resume so that I wouldn't overqualify myself. I sent out 400 in three months; 3% responded for interviews. I got no real positive feeling from any of these. First you see the personnel officer, then some vice president. Everyone's pleasant. Sorry comes in a letter, and you don't even know who wrote it.

I started to worry about age. The qualifications are there, the experience. What's holding things back? Should I go into business at age 62? What for? Who would I leave it to? I've got two daughters; neither son-in-law is going to go in with me. I got down in the dumps.

Daniel also tried the state employment service and some of the nonprofit agencies serving older people.

They are all the same, try to build up your morale. They give you the book of job listings to go through. You send out your resumes. But the agencies don't even know whether the listings are still current or have been filled. There's no follow-up.

I decided to try for something working for the state and went to state personnel. First you send in a resume. Then they call you to come in and fill out an application. Then you get an appointment for an interview forty-five, sixty, ninety days later, just an interview, not for any particular job.

One night Daniel went to a party given for a cousin who was celebrating his eightieth birthday. Until then, Daniel never had given a thought to calling on his cousin, a prominent accountant who had run for public office and was likely to have a wide acquaintanceship in the business community.

I told him I was looking for work. He said, I'll look around for you. He called me the next night and said, "Call so-and-so." I did, and went in to see my present employer. They're in the second mortgage business. It's a small outfit, two full-time, two part-time employees. The other full-time employee is a woman of 59 or 60. The boss is about the same age. They asked me what I wanted. I said $22,000; I was afraid to ask for more. He said, OK, we'll start you at twenty-two with a raise in six months and pension vesting in five years. I've been there a year. I started with eight sets of books, now I've got eleven. It's interesting; I like it fine.

Why didn't he call his cousin earlier? "It never dawned on me."

Networking Without Design

Other job seekers had the right connections to the right networks but never realized how useful these contacts could be. Barbara D. found both the jobs she won after age 50 through her social connections. But she never deliberately used her friends and acquaintances to build a network. If she had, she might have saved herself months of frustration.

Barbara had an M.A. in nutrition, had worked briefly for pay, and put in many years of volunteer work with children, while raising her own family. She found herself a widow at 50, when the youngest two of her six children were still in high school. Her husband, who had been a physician and a medical school professor, left her with no immediate financial worries. A year later she began to feel the urge to do something constructive and started looking around.

Her first job happened by itself. She was sitting next to a graduate school dean, a fellow parent, watching a hockey game at the private school her children attended. He asked what she was up to, and she told him she was looking for employment.

He asked me to come in and see him about working for him. What for? I said. I can't do secretarial work.

That wasn't what he wanted. "I need someone whose head is screwed on right to help me with a project," he told me. I worked there full-time for four years and I loved it. When the project ended, there was nothing else unless you had a Ph.D. or an M.B.A. I didn't think it was realistic to go to graduate school at my age.

Looking for work was devastating. At first I stayed with the academic community because that was what I was familiar with. But I was either overqualified or underqualified.

I was surprised at the reaction of people my own age. For example, my brother-in-law asked me, Why are you trying to find a job? You don't have to work. Other people thought it was cute. It bothered me. I thought I had something to contribute, that my talents weren't being used as they could be.

A friend at a cocktail party gave her an introduction to someone at the local bank.

I was interviewed by an M.B.A. in a mannish suit who probably got her degree three years ago. I'm presentable, dress well, look younger than my years. She said: "Well, now, what would you like to do?" I told her I wanted to do community outreach, and I explained why and what I thought I had to offer. She said, we have M.B.A.s for that.

Barbara also applied at a hospital for a position as director of volunteers.

The young woman who interviewed me spent the whole time telling me her woes. At the Red Cross, for the same kind of job, a young thing in sneakers, sipping her coke, said, "Oh you'd be good organizing the Bloodmobile." She saw me as a suburban matron. She didn't take me seriously.

"I had all kinds of connections, but I never got help from any of them," she told us. In fact, except for the people with whom she had worked in her first job, and the chance encounter at a cocktail party, she never called on them. She expected, perhaps hoped, that they would call her.

> I had begun to think I had no marketable skills. My first boss warned me that I'd probably seem threatening to some people who would be afraid I was after their job. Yet I find younger people better to work with than older ones. I talked to one older man who said, "There are lots of people around like you. You probably won't find a job."

At last she met a woman socially who was president of a newly formed nonprofit children's organization. Barbara had helped out as a volunteer there. After she had had a chance to present her ideas to the president, they took her on as a part-time staff consultant. They had very little money and didn't know how to get started. Barbara found she had the contacts and organizing ability to get them off the ground. She earns $16 an hour, and she can arrange her own work schedule.

Mutual Assistance

The first thing that happens to most people when they lose a job is that their self-esteem deflates like a balloon, and the last thing they feel like doing is asking someone who is working for a helping hand. Joining a support group with others in the same situation can provide the comfort, encouragement and guidance to recover confidence.

Nonprofit agencies sponsor support groups for all ages, but few are oriented towards older mid-level people. One job loser who joined a support group offered by a state job-match center told us:

> We were all mature people who had gone through a lot of job searching. I could help someone write a resume myself. But all the leadership comes from the staff. There should be some participation from people in the group. Why not have enough copies of everyone's resume to pass around to everyone and tap the resources of the group? There are only seven of us and we're in there twelve to fourteen hours. Each individual could have a half hour to say, "this is what I need help on most," and keep the discussion structured so you discuss just that.

Former members of the job support group for "midlife women" organized by a social service organization in New York City actually followed that pattern on their own. Seven members continued to meet privately for some months after the official workshop had ended. We interviewed four of them some time later, and they were enthusiastic about the benefits—not just the continuing support and encouragement from their peers, which all agreed were vital, but also the useful advice and contacts. "You walked out of there feeling human again," was the way one member put it.

Katherine B., an experienced executive secretary, was one of that group. She is single, 61, has no family to give her emotional or financial support. To be near her ailing mother, she had relocated to New York when she was 50, giving up the "ideal job."

Ten years with an investment counseling firm had their rewards. She worked hard and got raises. What she could not know was that the firm with the prestigious name had a fraudulent tax shelter. The SEC caught up with them. Katherine got two weeks' severance pay; the man who fired her got a seven-year prison sentence.

I read the *New York Times*, I went to agencies. I was looking for a place as an executive secretary. Then I lowered it to just secretary because I had to have some income.

Well, I must have gone on twenty interviews, good jobs, decent jobs. Not one of them selected me. When I took typing tests I did eighty-five words a minute. I'm an expert typist, I'm a good organizer. I have good judgment. I just had the feeling they didn't want someone older. I was told once or twice that I was overqualified.

The ads say things like "energetic," "corporate appearance," and all these little code words that make you realize that if you went there you'd get short shrift. Occasionally they say "mature," but those are the lower paying jobs. So I took a temporary job. I got a long-term one and I stayed there eight months. It paid $8 an hour, which is about $6 after taxes, but no security. I didn't know from week to week if I was going back. And no health benefits.

It was a desperate period. I was going through the ads every day and finally I found something. I went up there—it was a scientific institute—and they decided to hire me. It only pays $16,000—that's $8000 a year less than I had been earning—but it has good health benefits and there is a pension and annuity after you have been there three years. It's grant money, though, and it ends in July 1987. I may have to take early retirement and that worries me because I don't know how I'm going to live on my social security.

During her most depressed period, Katherine joined the support group.

We met once a week for eight weeks, and our little group was so congenial that we decided to continue on our own. We carried on for four or five months longer, and it was most helpful. I got assistance writing my resume, hints about where to look. We passed each other's resumes around to our own contacts, made suggestions about how to present ourselves.

Besides discovering that other people were having the same difficulties, I found a job. One woman in the group wasn't so much looking for work as for emotional support. She was the president of an art society, and wanted someone to work for the society on weekends. She asked me if I would be interested, so I'm doing that too.

I went into the group with an open mind, but I didn't really expect much from it. I found a friend and a part-time job, all in one person. The idea of the support group is very, very good. In fact, I'm thinking of joining another one.

Having It All Through Outplacement

A few job losers we spoke to were offered outplacement services provided by specialized agencies to help them renew their careers, paid for by the employers who dismissed them. One man found his outplacement service experience in New York City useless and demeaning. The others, two men and a woman, gave high praise to two Boston area organizations.

Outplacement agencies do not provide referrals to jobs. The best ones offer testing, counseling, confidence building, a place to job hunt from in an atmosphere designed to build confidence. They help develop and reinforce job seekers' ideas about the direction their search should take. The two exemplary agencies we heard about put no time limit on their services; users stayed with them until they found a job. One agency keeps in touch with graduates after they find employment. The cost to the employer-client is about 15% of the terminated employee's former salary.

Like other services, outplacement ranges from very good to very bad: Edgar M. had never heard of an outplacement agency when, at 52, he lost his job as vice president of a prominent financial house in New York City following a buyout. But he was willing to give it a try. Edgar may be exaggerating his negative experience; he was certainly not in a receptive frame of mind. On the other hand, the agency his employer enlisted to help him seems to have relied primarily on testing rather than using tests as one of many tools in an individually tailored program.

It was degrading and humiliating, the worst experience I've ever had. The whole environment, up there every day with a half dozen middle-aged men, no privacy, elbow to elbow. My firm hired them to get me out of their sight. You pay us, we'll keep him up here.

It was a month before they did anything to help me put together a resume. They spent all their time taking my life history, asking me my interests, giving me tests. "We'll have our psychologist spend time to see what you're fitted for." Gave me aptitude tests, even the ink-blot test.

I had been successful and highly respected; they made me feel inferior. They didn't give me a single suggestion on how to take my skills and use them in a new environment. They weren't realistic about the age problem, either. They told me to come in and call people I knew, network. I can do that at home.

The Right Stuff

Lawrence R., also in his early fifties, found the outplacement service he used extremely helpful. "Anyone who's been relieved of his duties and doesn't have this service is cheated."

Formerly the general manager of a brush manufacturing company, he had been forced to leave with three days' notice when a new and younger president took over. The company hired an outplacement firm to help him find a new position, and he drove twenty-three miles to its offices every day for ten months.

> This was the second period of unemployment in my entire working life. You can sell a product but you don't know how to sell yourself. The outplacement service gives a boost to your self-esteem—mine was pretty low. Everybody there was in the same boat, all of them outstanding people. The men were in their 50s, the women in their 40s.
> They help you, talk about what's happened to them, like no one returning your calls. There were five of us who talked together, lunched together every day. We persuaded the head of the agency to have Friday morning coffee with us.

Through these discussions, Lawrence faced the reality that brush manufacturing is a declining industry, and that his age would be a problem in resuming his career. He realized he needed to break into a new field. The support of a permanent group of people in a similar situation, whom he saw every day, kept up his morale as one day followed another without results.

> Working there on job search was a real advantage. If you stay home you waste time on personal chores. I went there 9 to 4 the first few months, then 9 to 2. You have your own private cubicle. I'd go through the ads. All the publications you need are right there. They give you a questionnaire to make you come up with what it is you really want to do.

Much of the day was spent on networking.

> I met fine people. Only two of eighty I called were unwilling to meet with me for an information interview. You have to get to the presidents and chairmen of the board; personnel officers don't mean anything.

You are looking for information and advice, not a job.

I chatted with my next-door neighbor, and he arranged an interview with a chief executive officer. That man was looking for someone with a different background. But he was a member of the Young Presidents' Association, and he said there's so and so, he might help, and then there's so and so.

He gave me twenty-one leads, and I followed up. One actually made a job offer, but the compensation was too low and the commuting was an hour and twenty minutes. I saw six CEOs, and each one sends you to four contacts.

Things started to dry up, and I went back to my neighbor. He gave me the name of another fellow and that opened it up again. One was gung-ho over the phone, but when I got to his office he apologized: he's not hiring. Can I use your name? No. Another CEO, who was very difficult to talk to over the phone, invited me in and gave me suggestions when I went to see him. He telephoned right then and there and arranged two appointments. Now I play tennis with him. It reinforces your belief in human nature.

Answering a blind ad turned the trick in the end. Lawrence accepted the job—district manager for an out-of-state company selling large recreational equipment. His job-loss experience was

very humbling. I never liked firing people—who does—and now I'm going to put the emphasis on awards for good work rather than threats for mistakes. And I'll be goddamned if I don't have personnel phone the people they see who aren't hired!

It took Connie W., 61, seven months to find "a fabulous job" as administrator with a large firm of professionals at an "executive level salary" that represents an increase over her last one. She found the job on her own, but she gives the outplacement service credit for providing the essential support.

She and her husband had run their own business until his death nine years earlier, leaving her with four children. She went to work for a syndication company, starting at $9,000 a year. A self-taught computer expert, she put the accounting and office functions on line. After eight years, the work lost its challenge for her, and she decided to leave. At her request, her employer provided outplacement service.

> When you leave a job, you're cut off from a large piece of your life. It's a shock. That's where I found the outplacement service very important. There's a support group of professionals here for you—you have a home. Every Monday the job searchers met together. It was fascinating. They like to tell you how they got their interviews, and it motivates others to hear them, share their problems. You see yourself on TV, and the feedback about myself gave me confidence.
>
> I loved looking for a job. It's a learnable skill. I didn't have it when I started. I looked four to five hours a day, and I found it fascinating to talk to people. The agency doesn't do the work for you. They gave me good support in figuring out what I wanted to do, how to go about finding it.
>
> You take a personality test. You design your ideal company, what things matter, who you can talk to. I found out that I was an extrovert. I learned that the person I work for is very important to me, and that I like to work on my own. They ask you to list fifty people you know, twenty target companies you might like to work for. The church I belong to gave me fifty people to network with as a start.
>
> I actually turned down three offers. I knew the CEO at my present firm casually, and I went to see him. He said, You want to talk to the executive director, and I did. It turned into a job interview.

Raising Standards

Although high-priced outplacement does not guarantee high quality, low-cost service from a for-profit
agency is almost certain to be shoddy. The agencies that
Lawrence R. and Connie W. found so helpful charge
several thousand dollars for each participant. Some
outplacement firms charge only a few hundred dollars.
Most employers who offer outplacement to anyone below the top executive level will be tempted by bargains.
Clients get what they pay for, but job hunters don't
always get what they want. Low quality service can do
more harm than good by demoralizing job seekers and
devaluing search techniques that might have been
useful.

There is nothing about the networking techniques
used in outplacement that requires a high-priced setting
or makes them applicable to top-level jobs only. Contacts in high positions are good for networking but not a
prerequisite. Not everyone has access to a pillar of the
church or a chairman of the board, but everyone knows
somebody—a relative, friend, neighbor, former coworker or boss—who could be the first link in a chain.

With the right kind of guidance, the staff of nonprofit
agencies can provide training in identifying contacts, in
information interviewing, and other networking skills.
In Chapter Ten we suggest how quality outplacement
could be provided to middle-level people at reasonable
cost.

Networking abc's are also spelled out in Chapter Ten.
The strategies are very simple. The reason for emphasizing them is that most mid-level and higher jobs are
obtained through networking. Most of our interviewees
did not network, except very casually. Although using
the strategy does not guarantee finding a job, not using

it will probably prolong the search and make it less fruitful.

The first steps are the hardest. Not the pen and pencil work of developing prospect lists, but the initial overtures for information interviews, explained in Chapter Ten. Rehearsing the request before making it, preferably with someone who acts the part of your potential contact, can break the ice and improve the pitch. Training in information interviewing at a career or employment agency is also helpful.

It is never too late to join and become active in one or more of the networks that operate in every community, including the chamber of commerce, small business groups, professional and trade associations, women's organizations. Nonmembers are usually welcome to attend a meeting or two on a trial basis. Locating these groups is no problem. Some publicize their meetings in the newspaper. Friends and colleagues, past and present, will know of others. Public libraries have directories of national organizations that can supply names and addresses of their local branches.

5 | FIGHTING BACK

"Yes, it is unlawful to discriminate in employment according to age, but who is going to get caught? How to collect evidence? It is impossible unless the potential employer is foolish enough to violate the statutes by actually asking your age and you get it recorded on a hidden tape recorder."

These lines from a letter published in the *Boston Globe* for July 23, 1986, convey the hopelessness and frustration of an unemployed middle-aged school teacher who has repeatedly seen himself and other qualified candidates over 40 passed over in favor of people in their 20s. The lines also reflect a general need on the part of older workers for better information and expert advice on how to exercise the right to protection from age discrimination in employment under the federal law, the Age Discrimination in Employment Act (ADEA), and the antidiscrimination legislation now in effect in most states.

This chapter provides some background information on the federal law and the way it has been used. We discuss the options an individual has when considering an age discrimination charge against an employer: whether to employ a lawyer and seek redress through the courts, or rely on a state or federal enforcement agency. The outcomes in some concrete cases are also presented.

What the Law Provides

The United States is almost alone in the world in having age discrimination legislation on its books, and experience with it is still brief. In 1965, when a study by the Department of Labor found that unemployment among older workers was growing, and that 50 percent found themselves discriminated against in their efforts to stay on the job, President Lyndon Johnson called on Congress to remedy "the serious and senseless loss" of the nation's human resources.

Congress passed the ADEA in 1967, virtually without opposition. It was a by-product of the prevailing general sentiment against discrimination, of public acceptance of the idea that people should be judged on their merits, and that men and women who had worked hard all their lives had a vested interest in their job. Unlike Title VII of the Civil Rights Act on which it was modeled, it had no popular movement or pressure group behind it pushing for congressional action. The middle-aged did not take to the streets, and for more than a decade they made little use of the law.

Originally, the ADEA protected workers aged 40 to 65, in the same way that Title VII of the Civil Rights Act protects women and minorities, against discrimination in hiring, firing, job placement and promotion. It was amended in 1978 to cover people up to the age of 70. Since 1986, when Congress eliminated mandatory retirement at any age, there has been no upper age limit. In 1979 responsibility for enforcement was transferred from the Labor Department to the Equal Employment Opportunities Commission (EEOC).

Although the number of charges of age discrimination filed with the federal government is still considerably less than the volume of complaints involving race and sex, it has risen sharply in recent years—from 5,300 in 1979 to 11,000 in 1982, and 17,700 in 1984. These figures, stories in business journals about "staggeringly large age discrimination verdicts," and claims that juries (which are not provided for in sex and race discrimination suits) have a built-in bias in favor of an older plaintiff, may give the impression that older workers are on a suing spree and are cleaning up. This is far from the truth.

Who Goes to Court

The cases that reach court, whether brought privately by the plaintiff or sometimes by the EEOC on behalf of a group of complainants, represent only a fraction of total charges lodged with the federal antidiscrimination agency.

The cost of suing is high (several thousand dollars), the wait for a decision is long (four to five years), and the mental anguish protracted. The stakes must be high enough to make it worthwhile. Men who have climbed to the top or near it are used to litigation and have the most to gain, as do their lawyers. About 80% of private suits are brought by white male executives and professionals in the upper salary brackets.

There have been some spectacular victories. Eugene Goodman, an international marketing executive, won a case against his employer after he was passed over four times in favor of younger men for a vice presidency he

HOW TO RECOGNIZE DISCRIMINATION

The following are some warning signs, not necessarily proof, of discrimination. They may prompt
you to start collecting evidence.

In hiring:
- After expressing interest in your qualifications by
  mail or phone, a prospective employer rejects
  you following an interview because you are overqualified, or "we aren't hiring just now."
- An employer advertises for "recent college graduates" or people with three to five years experience.
- You are asked your age, when you plan to retire,
  whether you have health problems, whether you
  mind working with younger people.
- A younger person with the same (or poorer)
  qualifications is hired instead of you.

On the job:
- You are passed over for promotions for which you
  are qualified in favor of younger employees.
- You are denied training opportunities that are
  available to younger staff members.
- You receive a lower salary than younger workers
  doing the same or less responsible work.
- You are denied health insurance or other benefits
  because of age.
- You are transferred without cause, suddenly
  start receiving poor performance evaluations,
  your supervisor or fellow employees make derog-
  atory remarks about older people in your presence.
- You are demoted or some of your work is assigned to younger employees.

In job termination:
- You were laid off when younger employees were retained, when your pension was about to vest, within a few years of full pension or when you refused early retirement.

had been promised. It took him six years and his life savings, but he was granted an award of $452,400 by jury and in 1983 published his litigation experiences in a book titled *All the Justice I Could Afford.*

It is extremely hard for an individual job applicant who has not been hired because of age to document discrimination, because he or she is rarely told why they failed to get the job and who did get it. Even if the interviewer lets something slip, the applicant does not have a hidden recorder to tape the evidence.

A discriminatory hiring policy may be more successfully demonstrated by a group of workers in a "class action suit," which may be brought when a number of employees are in a similar situation.

More than 500 applicants for production-line jobs with Goodyear Rubber won their case against the company's Tennessee plant. It refused to hire workers over 40 on the grounds that the work was too strenuous for them: They would not be as productive as younger workers, and company profits would suffer.

The plaintiffs showed that another Goodyear plant hired workers over 40, and that their performance records were equal to or better than those of younger ones. Goodyear Tennessee had to change its policy.

Most age discrimination lawsuits charge unlawful firing, and here too there have been some dramatic awards in group suits. For example:

The court ordered United Airlines to pay $18 million

in damages to 112 pilots and flight engineers who had been required to retire when they reached the age ceiling of 60, instead of being transferred to other jobs where there was no ceiling.

Three employees won a sizable victory against I. Magnin department store in San Francisco when their lawyers were able to produce reports by company executives declaring that there were too many superannuated people on the staff, and articulating a company policy of jazzing up the San Francisco store's image with bright young managers. The three were all in their early 50s at the time they were fired in 1978.

The six-week trial brought out, among other things, that in its 40-year history almost no one had ever remained with I. Magnin long enough to qualify for a pension, a fact the company claimed was pure coincidence. The three litigants did not get their jobs back. But in 1983 they collected $1.9 million in damages plus $400,000 in fees and costs.

Enforcement Agencies

The vast majority of individuals who seek redress for age discrimination rely entirely on the free services of the federal and state enforcement agencies. In states that have their own antidiscrimination laws, the federal and state laws are virtually identical in all important respects. In these states, EEOC is authorized to contract with the state agency to handle some of its age discrimination cases.

This can be an advantage for complainants, since EEOC maintains only forty-eight area offices (one for all of New England, for example) and is so short staffed due to lack of funding and other support from Washington that it has a huge backlog of cases awaiting resolution. State agencies may be able to process complaints more rapidly. The Massachusetts Commission Against Discrimination (MCAD), for example, maintains four offices at different locations in the state.

A charge may be filed either with the EEOC or with the state agency, provided the respective agency's rules about time limits are met. In either instance, the case is automatically registered with the other agency as well, and one informs the other of its findings.

Whichever agency undertakes to handle the charge, the procedure is substantially the same. The agency investigates and may find "probable cause for crediting the allegations" or "lack of probable cause." If the finding is "probable cause," the agency will hold a conference with complainant and employer and attempt to arrive at a conciliation agreement. If no cause is found, the complainant can ask for reconsideration and, if the negative finding is upheld, he or she still has the option of retaining a lawyer and filing suit in court.

In some cases no official finding is made, but the commission succeeds in mediating a settlement that is accepted by both sides. The agency is *not* obliged in every case to determine whether or not an employer has violated the law.

In age discrimination cases, whether they involve an employer's decision not to hire or promote an older person, or a decision to fire him or her, and whether the charge is heard by an agency or by a court, the complainant must prove that age was the determining (not necessarily the only) factor in the employment action. If she or he can show this, it is then up to the employer to account for the decision by citing reasonable factors other than age, such as proven deficiencies in performance or conduct, or economic imperatives. The burden of proof then shifts back to the complainant, who must demonstrate that these were not the real reasons but were pretexts for discrimination.

WHEN YOU DECIDE TO TAKE ACTION

- Consider raising the issue first with your employer in a nonthreatening way.
- Consider making use of the company's grievance procedure if it has one.
- Write to the AARP, Worker Equity, 1909 K Street N.W., Washington, D.C. 20049, and the Older Women's League, 1325 G Street N.W., Washington, D.C. 20005, for their booklets on age discrimination in employment.
- Weigh the risks and benefits: Does the relief you might receive justify the time, effort, and possible mental anguish?
- If you are unsure, obtain legal advice. Ask your local bar association whether they have a referral service and, if not, how you can obtain a low-cost consultation.
- If you decide to file a charge with the EEOC or your state agency, don't delay. You must do so within 180 days of the discriminatory event, 300 days in states with antidiscrimination laws.
- Phone your local EEOC office for directions. Call your state agency as well, as requirements may differ.
- You must file your charge in writing, giving names and the details of the alleged discrimination.
- Ask the agency where you file your charge when you can expect to hear from them, and what the next steps will be. If you don't hear, phone and inquire.
- Usually a charge is investigated. A conference may then be held at which the investigator attempts to reach a settlement. Remember that the agency is not *obliged* to determine whether the employer violated the law.
- If mediation fails, the investigator will decide

whether to investigate further, refer the case for legal action, or close it.

- If your charge is rejected, you will be notified of the period within which you may appeal.
- If your appeal is refused, you still have the option of filing a lawsuit within ninety days.
- Should you decide at the start to bring a private lawsuit, you must nevertheless first file a charge with the EEOC and wait sixty days before going to court. You may not delay more than two years (three, in some cases). Remember that lawsuits are expensive. Some lawyers accept cases on a contingency basis. Most require fees up front.

Reluctance to Act

Only three of our interviewees initiated a lawsuit. All were related to dismissal. The case of one of these, Stephen M., is described below. One other was settled in the complainant's favor, and the third was still pending at the time this was written.

About a dozen other interviewees turned to the MCAD for assistance following dismissal. Some had thought about doing so but were held back by fear of being blackballed by employers as troublemakers or of losing their case and being subjected to employer retaliation. Many were also reluctant to relive an unpleasant experience.

Jane E., 54, was employed as a research biochemist in a hospital, earning $16,000 a year.

After learning that the project she was working on was about to run out of funds, she spoke to the personnel office about finding another position.

He sent me for interviews where he knew I didn't qualify. I'd see job postings that I was qualified for and

go after them, but they would already be filled. I'd ask
the department heads why they hadn't contacted me.
They said they never got my file from personnel.

Jane accused the personnel officer of discrimination
against her. Younger people, she told him, were getting
jobs that she could fill. Why hadn't he referred her to
them?

He let slip that he was worried about his own job.
The head of the hospital was making big cutbacks,
hiring young people at lower rates who'd maybe stay a
year or two.

She had taken her complaint about age discrimination to the company officer she held responsible, but
when this failed to produce results she went no further.
She did not consider contacting MCAD or EEOC. She
looked for and finally found a position with another
institution, although she would have much preferred to
remain at the hospital.

High Rejection Rate

The few interviewees who did take their cases to the
Massachusetts state agency were unclear about what
was expected of them. No one had explained to them
what constituted proof of age discrimination. They did
not understand the basis on which the commission's
decision had been made. They did not realize that a
major aim of the MCAD is conciliation, and that this
usually brings about a settlement that falls short of
what the complainant thinks they deserve.

In trying to follow their cases, we found ourselves
equally confused. Our researches did not succeed in
uncovering what the criteria were for accepting a
charge, for attempting conciliation, for finding "proba-

ble cause," or any consistency in the way cases were handled. We concluded that it depended largely on the individual investigator's competence and motivation.

We found that in a very high percentage of cases brought to the MCAD, the complainant's charge of age discrimination is not upheld. In 1985, 402 cases of age discrimination were registered with the Massachusetts commission (and automatically with the area office of the EEOC). Of the 192 that had been disposed of in the Boston office by May of the following year, only 44 (23%) decisions brought any relief to the complainant. Among them were cases that the commission had conciliated without a finding, and others that were settled in discussions between lawyers for the two sides, not by the commission.

Seventy-seven cases, or almost 40%, were rejected by the MCAD for "lack of probable cause." Thirty-three more were simply registered with the MCAD as a condition for filing a lawsuit; the plaintiff had decided at the start to hire a lawyer and initiate suit. The rest were withdrawn or dropped for a variety of technical reasons. The percentages parallel closely the disposition of all discrimination cases (including race, sex, and handicap) by the MCAD in the years 1983–85. "Probable cause" was found in only 4% of cases.

The men and women we talked to who had asked the state to intervene on their behalf received token relief at best. In no case was the employer actually found to have violated the law.

Inconsistent Treatment

Flora D., whose story is related in Chapter Two, complained to the MCAD that her employer advertised for and hired a younger replacement for her without even notifying her, that previous to this two older employees had been fired, and that a vice president of the company had made remarks of the "let's get some young faces around here" variety in the presence of several older employees, of which she was one.

MCAD discouraged her from filing charges on the grounds of insufficient proof. She was told that she would need to show at least five other people fired and then five younger people hired. Similar advice was given to another older woman, employed by the city, who claimed she had been consistently passed over for promotion. She would have to find five others who had been denied the chance to move up.

Clara P. had a very different experience. A part-time evening supervisor at a church-affiliated nursing home, she was 74 when she and a somewhat younger coworker, Blanche, were fired without notice "for economy reasons." When she wrote to her administrator's supervisor, she was offered a daytime shift, which she did not want.

Clara and her friend were convinced that age was behind their dismissal, and they went to the MCAD as a matter of principle. After talking with the field investigator, Blanche wanted to back out. It was the MCAD representative who insisted on going ahead. Through mediation, without a finding of wrongdoing, she obtained a settlement of several weeks' pay for each.

Paul B. was another who received a sympathetic hearing. Paul, the head of a hospital laboratory, was fired at age 42 after twenty years service, good performance reviews, and raises. Suddenly, in July 1985, three unfavorable reviews followed in rapid succession. He was unable to find out what his shortcomings were, and he was terminated after he refused to resign. Two other members of his department also lost their jobs.

At the EEOC he was told that he had no case. But a field investigator at the MCAD felt it was worth making an effort, and was able to negotiate an additional two months' severance pay for him.

Misunderstood Effort

Albert W.'s case illustrates how confusing the role of the MCAD can be to the uninformed citizen, so that well-intentioned intervention on behalf of the complainant goes unappreciated.

The graphics manager of a small press, which was in turn a division of a larger company, Albert came to the MCAD charging age discrimination and breach of contract. His written statement set forth what he considered unfair behavior and mismanagement, rather than documenting age discrimination. His chief complaint was that the difference between his earnings and those of the production workers he supervised did not reflect the difference in responsibilities. Moreover, the gap had been shrinking over the years as a result of wage increases won by the workers.

Albert was told that since he was 71 he was no longer in the protected age group and that the law did not apply to him. (This was before Massachusetts declared mandatory retirement at any age illegal and thus removed the age cap of 70 from the state age discrimination law.)

In spite of this, the commission mediated the dispute and arrived at a settlement, "without entering a finding as to the merits of the allegations." Albert got a 10% raise retroactive to the time he filed his complaint, plus a 2% bonus on any earnings of the composition shop over $150,000 a year. He felt he had "lost," however, because the raise had been "due him for years" and because his other complaints were not addressed.

Retaining a Lawyer

Two job losers we interviewed received financial set-
tlements as a result of negotiations between lawyers for
the two sides. Their cases had been registered with the
MCAD, as required, before the plaintiff's lawyer could
proceed. Beyond that, the agency played no part in the
settlement. Yet their cases are among those listed by the
MCAD as having obtained relief through it.

Harold K., 56, a salesman of foundry products, had
worked for a steel company for just one year when he
was terminated on the grounds that he was not showing
results and that the territory did not justify a salesman.
He was told that he was not being replaced. A few weeks
earlier, however, he had received a letter from the president of the company congratulating him on a job well
done. He had been producing sales of $120,000 a month.

Shortly after leaving, he discovered that his job had
been given to a 30-year-old with no outside sales experience who was, moreover, a friend of someone else in the
company. "It was a shoo-in. They just wanted to get
someone cheaper." He found a lawyer to take his case on
a contingency basis and obtained damages of $15,000.

Elizabeth C.'s view is that "MCAD is a joke. They
didn't give me any help. I think the whole thing should
be exposed."

She had worked for an international lumber company for ten years, and was secretary to the comptroller
when the company was sold. The new owner in Texas
was obviously interested in slimming the operation. The
comptroller group was ordered to absorb computer operations that had previously been done elsewhere, but
they were not permitted to hire any help. Elizabeth,
then 60, took a course in computers and passed with top
marks. "It was just unbearable. We were working round
the clock."

Her boss left in disgust, and his replacement arrived.

There was something very wrong with him. He wouldn't talk to anybody, refused to read his mail, refused to take any calls. He boasted that he was a professional hit man, and he as much as told us that he had been hired to get rid of the whole comptroller's group we worked for. He had a list on his desk. I saw the names and I should have Xeroxed it. I'm sorry now that I didn't.

He called me in one day and said, how fast can you take dictation? Take this, and he rattled it off as fast as he could talk. This is what first made me suspicious. Thank God I got it all and brought it back. How fast can you type? About eighty words a minute, I said. Type this. I did, and brought it back.

When he couldn't find fault with my secretarial work he said, "From now on you're going to do accounting." In the meantime he had fired one of the accountants. I said, "I don't know anything about accounting."

"Well, you'll have to if you're going to be my assistant."

He started being absolutely miserable to me and also to another women of about 55 who had been there twenty-five years and actually did the assistant comptroller's work. He said, "You know my former secretary, I used to harrass her so that she'd go to the ladies room and throw up." He laughed. He kept after both of us, but neither of us would quit.

On other occasions he shouted at Elizabeth and used foul language. One day he called her in and asked her to sign a prepared statement of dismissal on grounds of incompetence.

I said "I'm not signing that. I'm not incompetent." He said, "Well you'll sign it or you won't get severance pay or anything." I said "I'm not doing anything, you can see my lawyer." Then he calmed down and said just pick up your things and go, which I did. I asked, "What about my vacation and severance pay?" He said, "You're not getting anything."

When Elizabeth went to collect her unemployment benefits, she found she could not get them because her boss had reported that she had been fired for incompetence.

> I had to get a lawyer. I had been to the MCAD, but the investigator told my lawyer that they went to the company and they couldn't get any evidence that it was age discrimination. The investigator never interviewed me or asked me any questions.
>
> In order to make the settlement I had to withdraw my case from the MCAD. My lawyer got together with their lawyers. I had done work for their lawyers and they liked me. I think they were afraid to have it come to court.

Elizabeth received $11,600, and the statement that she was incompetent was removed from her personnel records.

She now has a job with a high technology company. She had to take an $80-a-week cut, and she supplies secretarial services to two directors and their departments.

> I really tramped the streets, and I wouldn't have got this job if those two men had not been through the age thing themselves.
>
> I just had to get in out of the cold. I'm all alone; I don't have any family. It was such a traumatic experience I thought I'd have a nervous breakdown. I was so upset that I wanted out of the whole thing. I didn't want to face that man in court. I didn't want to see him again.

Elizabeth did not allow herself to be intimidated into quitting, and she did obtain legal advice.

The experiences of two managerial-level workers, Stephen M. and Dorothy V., illuminate the contrast between the course of events when the complainant retains a lawyer and when he or she relies entirely on a government enforcement agency.

To Sue or Not to Sue

Stephen M., now 67, is a research chemist with many patents and publications to his credit, whose story is told in Chapter Two. He had refused to take advantage of his company's "voluntary severance plan." When it was made plain to him that his job was being eliminated, and that there was to be a major layoff, after which there would be no position for him, he reluctantly signed a retirement agreement in February 1982, and immediately called his lawyer. In a thirty-seven page memorandum submitted to the court, Stephen's attorney argued that his client had been coerced into signing by the implementation of the company's plan to reduce the number of older people in its employ. His job had not been eliminated; he had been replaced by a younger (and cheaper) man.

One advantage of a lawsuit is that the pretrial procedure provides for obtaining information that complainants could not get on their own. The company claimed that Stephen had taken voluntary retirement after receiving an unsatisfactory rating from his supervisor, with whom he had a "steadily deteriorating relation." Stephen's lawyer obtained statements taken under oath from company executives that refuted the employer's version of Stephen's relations with his superiors and the circumstances surrounding his departure.

His lawyer also acquired a transcript of the speech by the vice president and CEO to the upper level meeting where this officer had presented the company policy calling for the departure of salaried workers near or over 55. He made it clear that pressure was to be used on them: "Let's not be brutal, but let's not be too timid."

As we saw in Chapter Two, Stephen waited five years, but his patience was rewarded. He received a six-figure settlement in an out-of-court agreement, and also had the satisfaction of being vindicated.

Dorothy V. chose to turn to the state antidiscrimination commission, without a lawyer to represent her. She was 61 when she was "persuaded" to take early retirement from her job as director of communications at a large hospital. She had been employed there for twenty years when a much younger man was made administrator of four important departments, including hers, all headed by senior workers.

Harrassment of those four people started immediately. One department head and his key people lasted less than a year. The second stayed on for two. It was three years when I decided that my health and professional reputation were in jeopardy, and I agreed to take retirement in December 1984.

In her case, she told us, the administrator's harrassment took the form of vetoing her orders for equipment needed to upgrade the communications system, and then later ordering the same equipment himself, interfering with her budget-making process, downgrading her assistant, and going behind her back to deal with and antagonize outside agencies that she had always worked with successfully. When she complained to a superior, the harrassment stopped; the administrator turned solicitous and began to urge her to retire.

He said things like, "Wouldn't it be nice if you could retire?" I'd say "No, I have no intention of retiring." On another occasion he would ask, "Wouldn't it be nice to be free?" It went on like the Chinese water treatment, drip, drip, drip. Then I got a letter from the personnel department saying they had heard I was interested in retiring. I thought they were after me, but it turned out that my administrator had told them that.

Eventually Dorothy succumbed: "I hadn't been allowed to carry out my job properly for three years, and I was beginning to have health problems that the doctor said were stress-related." She had received a 10 percent raise (unusually high for the hospital) in October 1984, from $35,000 to $39,000. She was offered six months salary at that rate, and her pension was calculated as though she had retired at 65 instead of at 61, a retirement package that the hospital described as the most generous they had ever granted.

In the meantime, she discovered that the hospital had adopted the findings from an independent salary study that showed that her salary before the October raise had been about $10,000 below the market rate. A young and inexperienced man was brought in to replace her, at a starting salary of over $40,000. She felt she had been conned into retiring because of her age, and that if she were not a women she would have been retired at the top salary level, $45,000, after twenty-three years.

She took her case to the MCAD, charging both age and sex discrimination and was asked to write a one-page statement.

I heard nothing for two months, and I finally phoned them. Oh, we were just about to send the findings to you, they said. You don't have a case. Wait a minute, I said. I haven't had a hearing. Oh, we got all the information we need from the hospital. You didn't get along with anybody. I didn't get along with anybody? I was there for twenty-three years!

The commission sent her a finding of "lack of probable cause" and a five-page summary of her employer's rebuttal. This was based in large part on a negative evaluation made by a superior eight years earlier, to which she had replied. (She had attempted to obtain copies of these documents from the personnel department before leaving the hospital, but the papers had disappeared from her files.)

Dorothy appealed the MCAD's dismissal of her complaint on the grounds that her employer's statement seriously misrepresented the facts, and she received an appointment for a hearing by return mail. When she arrived, the lawyer for the hospital was already there.

The MCAD representative kept us waiting a full hour. Then he talked without stopping for forty-five minutes, repeating all the hospital had told him. He cited as proof that the hospital does not discriminate against older workers the fact that they have many employees over 40.

I said, "I haven't seen the company allegations but I have evidence of my own." He said he was not interested in seeing it. I had quite a file, but I didn't even get my briefcase open. I asked to leave my evidence with him. He said I could but that he wouldn't read it.

When he had finished he dismissed the hearing, noting that he had given me forty-five minutes even though it was his policy not to give more than thirty minutes to any one case.

At that point Dorothy could have appealed to the EEOC for a review. She knew that the two agencies worked together, and she thought it would be futile. She still had the option of hiring a lawyer and filing a lawsuit.

> I just didn't want to spend the time and emotions and money it would have cost. I wanted to turn my attention to building a new life.
>
> I'm more fortunate than most victims of discrimination. My reputation in my field is solid, and I have had more consulting work than I want offered to me since I retired. I have two other great satisfactions. One is that the man responsible for my retirement has since been substantially demoted. Also, the man who replaced me left the job after one year because he couldn't handle it.

Ten months after her case was dismissed by the MCAD, Dorothy received a form letter from the area EEOC office, declaring that it had examined the MCAD record and "found no reasonable cause to believe" that her charges were true. It notified her that she had a right to sue in federal court within ninety days. She did not avail herself of this, but she did send the EEOC area director a letter of complaint about the way her MCAD hearing had been conducted. The reply was another form letter reminding her that she had fifteen days in which to file this complaint after the conclusion of her hearing by the state agency, but that it was now too late.

In contrast to Stephen M., who retained a lawyer and initiated a suit, Dorothy V. handled everything herself, assuming that the state and federal antidiscrimination agencies were there to help her obtain fair play. Instead, she was put on the defensive by the state commission without the chance to answer the allegations made about her by her employer.

Reforms Require Funding

Although we did not know it at the time of our interviews, dissatisfaction with MCAD was mounting. During 1986 the Massachusetts State Legislature took up complaints about the inconsistency of MCAD's judgments regarding determination of "probable cause" to credit the allegations of the complaint. It found that no one knew exactly what these words meant, and that the commission lacked objective standards to aid investigators in making their decision.

A joint Senate–House bill that would clarify MCAD procedure was filed in 1986 and again at the beginning of 1987. As one civil rights lawyer testified at a joint committee hearing on the bill, "All too often, complainants are expected to produce definite evidence, while respondents' explanations are accepted without much investigation." In one case an investigator had told an attorney that she had been instructed "that she could not find probable cause unless the complainant's story of what happened was corroborated by a second witness."

The ad hoc committee of legal experts created by MCAD to advise it on changes, following criticism of its procedure, found that determination of "probable cause" was an invisible process that usually put the complainant at a disadvantage. Investigators who were not lawyers frequently made legal determinations on the outcome of a case.

It recommended that "probable cause" be found in all cases where the complainant's factual claim, if proved, would result in a finding of discrimination. Disputes over the facts should then be resolved at a hearing. It also proposed that the investigation process involve legal staff from the beginning.

Early in 1987 MCAD seemed about to make good on

its promise to amend its "probable cause" standard in line with the committee's recommendations and render legislation unnecessary. This could lead to an improvement in the prospects of complainants over what they were in 1985, the year in which our interviewees sought the state's assistance. They would be more likely to receive a finding of "probable cause," with a chance to present their case at a conference if the finding were contested by their employer. In case of a "lack of probable cause" finding, they or their attorneys would be able to present their objections at a public hearing.

How relevant are these Massachusetts experiences to other states? In a review of civil rights law enforcement in seven states including Massachusetts, conducted by the American Jewish Congress in 1984–85, agencies were found to be doing "a mediocre job" in discrimination cases of all types. The points on which the enforcement agencies were criticized were substantially the same as those raised by Massachusetts critics. The other states reviewed were Georgia, Michigan, Missouri, New York, Ohio, and Pennsylvania.

The airing of shortcomings is an important first step toward getting them corrected. Significantly better funding for civil rights enforcement agencies is essential, however, if they are to hire more and better trained staff and deliver more and better quality service.

Balancing the Scale

Most of our interviewees knew very little about their rights as older workers, or where to get information and advice, so they abandoned the idea of fighting back.

Employers, on the other hand, know a great deal about the antidiscrimination law. The organizations they belong to hold workshops and conferences on how to avoid discrimination charges by employees and job applicants. They receive newsletters, books, and other publications dealing with the issues. They know how to get more information if they need it. Until more older people become equally well-informed, the laws intended to protect them will continue to be breached.

Interviewees who did take action to protect their rights were also uninformed. They usually filed a complaint with the state antidiscrimination agency without legal or other counsel, expecting that the staff of the agency would inform and represent them. Instead, they received little or no help and scant redress. Interviewees who retained a lawyer were more successful.

Employers have staff, consultants, lawyers, to guide their defenses in age-discrimination lawsuits and agency proceedings. Those who bring the charges also need advisers and advocates but usually cannot afford the legal fees. There are ways of providing these people with competent, affordable consultation. We return to this point in Chapter Ten.

6 | BATTLE FATIGUE

Re-entry into the work world was difficult for almost all of our job losers. Only a few made it back to full-time, professional, management or technical jobs at close to the salary and level of the jobs they had lost. By the spring of 1986, when we last talked with them, many had made a partial comeback with hopes for bettering themselves. This chapter is about those others who, in spite of strenuous effort, had not been able to turn their luck around.

They were all men who had been unemployed for an unusually long time, in most cases several years. Several had recently taken, or were considering, part-time, low-level work. They had experienced crushing defeats since losing their last long-term position: rejection for positions they felt eminently qualified for, jobs they took a chance on that went sour, plummeting living standards, and the need to turn to relatives for help.

113

These repeated blows had severely damaged their self-confidence. Some had also lost faith in the ability of free enterprise to deliver on its promises, and not only because it had bruised them badly in their job searches. They also realized that systemic changes were under way that could prevent their reentry, except perhaps at the bottom, in the years ahead.

Still, with few exceptions, although wearied and discouraged, they had not surrendered completely.

The Steepest Plunge

Edgar M., at age 52, had held the highest paid position of any job loser we interviewed. He was making $88,000 a year plus a $20,000 bonus when he was forced out of an executive position on Wall Street. Two years later he was planning to sell his suburban home and move to another state, where his wife's family could provide inexpensive housing.

The event that started Edgar's descent was not unusual. The firm he worked for was sold.

Nothing happened for about eighteen months. Then a new president was appointed, and he started cleaning house, sweeping people out. One day the head of my division, a personal friend with whom I'd worked since I came there eight years earlier, called me in. He just said, we don't need you any more.

Edgar tried to change his friend's mind.

I told him there are fifty things I can do here.
"I have no choice," he said. "I must cut expenses."
"What about jobs in other divisions?"
"You can look," he said, "but you won't find anything."
He was right. You think you're set for the rest of your life, that your career depends on what you've

done for the firm. But certain generations get the shaft. Ours is the victim of corporate reorganization.

The firm did provide two rewards for service. They kept him on nominal salary for eighteen months so that he would have the ten years of employment necessary for his pension to be vested. Without that he would have had no pension rights. As it is, when he turns 65 in 1997, he will start getting $7,000 a year. In addition, he was offered the service of an outplacement agency, a demolishing experience for him, which we described in Chapter Four.

Spirit-Breaking

Like most of the men we interviewed, Edgar M. had experienced his first job-finding problem after a long career. He returned from service in the Korean war to work for twenty years at an investment company. He took his college degree at night.

> After about ten or twelve years I began moving up very fast. Then, in the early seventies, changes started at the top. A headhunter had been after me, saying I belonged on Wall Street. It was time to move on. I talked to eighteen people I knew about openings. One with a big investment firm, clicked. I offered just what they needed.

What Edgar wanted when he lost that position was "a full-time job where I could use my background in investment banking, corporate finance, and administrative management of support personnel and functions." He started his search on Wall Street, but

> it was a terrible time there. Still, my reputation was such that I thought I could walk into any firm. But I

wasn't what they wanted, a proven business-getter. I was an inside man.

He broadened his search to banks, insurance companies, Fortune 500 firms.

I had lots of friends and contacts, including CEOs. They weren't helpful; many of them said they were living on borrowed time themselves.

Was he asking too high a salary?

Salary never even came up. Every company was cutting back on people like me, cutting out middle management. People who start in their 20s get salary increases for twenty to twenty-five years and go up pretty high. Firms decide layers and layers are making more than they're worth, and they clean them out.

After ads, headhunters, and networking produced nothing, he tried commission sales.

I joined a small organization because I knew the person who ran it. I hadn't yet overcome my feelings of loss, so I didn't approach it with much enthusiasm. I soon learned that what they wanted couldn't be done because of legal prohibitions, and I left. All the time I was there I kept remembering what I used to be.

One haunting memory was of the new office he might have had.

The architect showed it to me one week before I lost my job. After years of a windowless office, I would have had a wonderful view. I couldn't get used to the closet I was working in. I kept thinking, I belong back there.

Edgar continued to broaden his search, and came agonizingly close to job offers. He answered an ad for a law firm administrator in an upstate city, for example, and got a call to an interview.

> I went with my wife, at the firm's invitation, all geared up with a feeling of hope. I met with the two partners for an hour and a half, one of the best interviews I ever had. Give us two weeks, they said. We've seen a lot of people and we haven't been impressed by any.

The rejection letter came two weeks later. "I'll never know if my age was the reason. They didn't know it when they invited me up because my resume doesn't show it."

Final Blows

Edgar's treatment from the employers in the city where he planned to relocate finally pushed him to admit defeat at least temporarily. He tried to line up job possibilities before he moved. His in-laws and other contacts arranged appointments at several companies, but it was the same old story. "The conversation was always friendly. They gave the impression they wanted to be helpful, would get back to me in a couple of weeks." None of them called, so Edgar called them. They had nothing.

Another tack also failed.

> I saw an article about a special program for older people at one of these companies, so I called the program director. She explained it was for people over 65. What about people in their 40s and 50s, I asked. She said I should send in my resume and she'd talk to personnel. She never got back to me although I called several times.

A third try at the same company, widely acclaimed for its exemplary older worker programs, produced the same results.

A friend called someone he knew there about a job opening, and told this person about me. He had two conversations with the guy and was then told I was overqualified, too good for them. I called the guy myself to say I was very interested. I can never get him on the phone. I leave messages, but he's never called back.

"I've decided to go out and be somebody else," he told us when we last talked.

I spent too long clinging to something that's gone. No use pretending you're what you were. That way, you'll never stop thinking about the past. Make a clean break.

Moving will cut our expenses in half. My wife is an experienced executive secretary and won't have any trouble getting a job, and I have a small pension from my first job. We could probably get by even if I don't work at all. Or maybe I'll take an entry-level job as a clerk.

I'm tired of battling with Corporate America, telling people how good I am, a two-year ordeal of getting my hopes up, for nothing but humiliation. I'm not going through life looking for something that just isn't there. You can't get a decent job in a major company after 45 or 50.

Carbon Copies

Edgar M. and Joseph T. lived several hundred miles from each other and spent their working lives in widely separated fields, but their stories parallel each other from start to finish. Joseph was also young, only 53, when he lost his middle-management job. He, too, had attended college at night as a young man while he worked days to get ahead. Joseph had been with his first employer, a well-known shoe manufacturer, for twenty-six years and then left for a better job, in his case for a position that did not require constant travel.

As in Edgar's case, corporate reorganization provoked his dismissal after eight years with his second employer, a large pharmaceutical company. It was purchased by a giant conglomerate and "sooner or later they threw out all the managers." Although Joseph's salary of $47,000 was much lower than Edgar's, it was considerably more than most of the job losers we interviewed had earned.

Joseph had managed systems development for the pharmaceutical company, and had had years of computer experience in his previous job. The market for his expertise was much stronger than for Edgar's.

> I looked everywhere, used all the classic methods. Why haven't I gotten a job? It's gotta be my age. I shaved down my resumes, cut out everything before 1963. That gets me interviews. Nothing follows. Employment and contract agencies call me in, smile, give me a big up. You call and they say they're working on it. Companies don't contact you after the first interview either, except a letter that says thank you, but no thank you.

Two years of fruitless job searching had convinced Joseph T. to break with his past. "I'm going to have to look in a different direction so I can do something with the rest of my life," he told us. He had sold his house months before and was living with relatives.

> You get very depressed if you let yourself. I can control my emotions by keeping busy. I go to the supermarket and do other stupid things like that. I read

a lot. Right now I'm helping a friend develop a computer program. I still answer ads. You have to keep your chin up.

Grasping at Straws

Gregory W. owned and ran a small real estate development firm until 1981 when it went under. He was 53. He tried to regain his footing in the development field, first as a consultant at $350 a day. When business turned out to be "spotty," he tried to find a position as a senior manager, asking for a salary of $75,000. "I called everyone I knew in the field. They had no place for me. Try so and so. Same answer."

Gregory's anxiety for a job made him less than cautious. About a year before we spoke with him, he answered an out-of-state ad that produced an interview and a job that he should have known better than to accept.

At the first meeting he was unable to learn much about the job or the company. "We're looking for someone to go into the Boston area and acquire real estate, no matter how long it takes," the interviewer told him. As to the company, "We're building mid-price condos up here, terrific president, vice president, etc. No financial facts. I got a rating that made them seem OK, but it came from people outside the company."

He was uneasy, but when he was asked to a second interview a week later, he went.

I thought I'd be seeing the president, but it was the same guy. We talked about salary. He said, $35,000. I said no. Then he offered $45,000 for six months, $50,000 after that, plus all expenses, a car, insurance. He said, "The president isn't here right now, I'll have to get authorization." I came back the next week. The president gave me two minutes. Rough, gruff, self-

made type in construction. I met the vp too. Another
rough diamond. Secretive. Steely eyed.

A week later, the president called him in for a meeting the next day. "We want a commitment from you. We
must get these properties." We agreed on salary. He
asked me to start in a week.

Gregory did. He rented an office, scouted for prop-
erty, using his own car, wrote up possibilities. After five
weeks he still had no salary or reimbursement for expenses. Then came a last-minute summons from the
president to a dawn breakfast. "We'll get you the car
next week and pay your health insurance. But the projects you're sending us are too high. Look outside
Boston." Gregory went out and reported possibilities.

An employment contract arrived after he had
worked about two months but no salary, car, or expenses. Gregory objected to several contract provisions,
was told to "pencil in the changes I wanted and mail it
back." The owner's son called him for a meeting a week
later. "We'll give you a week's salary and that's it. We're
not going into the Boston area." I asked about the pay
and expenses they owed me. They said we'll take care of
it.

They did not, until Gregory went to small claims
court.

It was a horribly disturbing experience after looking
so long. I had doubts from the start, but I was so eager.
Now I'm looking for $35–$40,000 jobs, I should have
done that long ago.

Reducing salary demands has not helped him so far.
When we last heard from him, he had just been turned
down for another development job.

I get a little brokerage work referred by friends. People like me, who've been on their own, have to work

harder on their contacts than I did at the beginning. I started too high, but I came down, and yet I'm not coming across to people. I don't know what the answer is.

Nothing Doing

"Hopeless," the job counselor told us when he suggested we interview Michael J., then 69. Michael had always worked in manufacturing. Nine months earlier he and 1,500 other employees of a high technology firm had been dismissed. He had been there nine years, was earning $33,000 as a senior production supervisor. "Manufacturing is dead right now," Michael said. "A million people younger than I are looking. All I can sell are the years of experience."

He obtained interviews, sometimes several at the same company, by answering ads, sending out resumes, visiting personnel offices and employment agencies. But employers were not interested.

> You never hear, or they tell you weeks later that the job is filled. Start-up companies should be able to use me. I'd take $20,000. I went to one place, they had resumes by the hundreds.

Michael is not in financial straits. He rents out half the two-family house he owns, and he and his wife both get social security.

> I'm not spending much time on looking any more. I play tennis, baby-sit with my grandchildren, keep busy. But you feel useless. I worked all my life since I came to the U.S. in 1938. I could still give a lot.

Long Shot

Kirk R. also worked in manufacturing, in his case the shoe industry. He was an early victim of structural change. At the time of our last conversation with Kirk, he was 58 and had been unemployed for three years. He had sold his house. "The money is running out," he said. "My folks have had to help me."

Kirk's career in the shoe industry had been stable if unspectacular. He worked for twenty-five years with a major company, and moved out of state when the company relocated. Then, fourteen years ago, it sold its plant. He was 44, making $17,000 in products development, "good money then. I got a job right away when I moved back to New England."

By then the industry was already in deep trouble, and Kirk as well. The project he was hired to develop fell through after six months. Jobs were hard to find, so in desperation he took one,

> a few steps back in responsibilities, almost the same salary, with a company that was going through bankruptcy, hoping it would straighten out. Instead, it fell apart. I started drinking more, couldn't find work for a year, outside or inside the shoe industry.

A start-up shoe company hired him, but let him go after a year.

> That's when I began working on my design for a sport shoe while I half-looked for work for another year. A company I tried to sell my design to wasn't interested but offered me a job in 1979 as manager of advanced product development at $26,000. When they got what they wanted, national recognition for a running merchandise line I developed, they invited me to leave.

Three years of unemployment followed. His eyesight had begun to fail.

I'd tell interviewers I could do it, whatever the job was, when I knew damn well I couldn't. I must have conveyed it, and blew possibilities. I had cataract operations on both eyes in 1982. They're fine now.

After surgery, Kirk received job-finding assistance from the state rehabilitation agency.

The program was good, they refer you to employers. Their weakness is contacts; they don't have good ones. They did encourage me on applying for a patent on my shoe design.

He turned to a service supported by the shoe industry to help workers and former workers find jobs within the industry.

They sent me on damn interesting interviews, several out of state. I thought sure I had the job several times. I don't know why I didn't get it.

Several places asked me if I minded working for people younger than I. I don't. They stereotype you as rigid at my age. People think young people have the ideas; old ones shoot them down. They don't believe you if you present the image of creative, advanced thinking when you're over 50. That's one reason I thought up something new.

Kirk R. still has hopes, however fragile.

My shoe patent just came through. Before applying I tried to sell the idea to development people inside companies, but they're a hard nut to crack. If it's a good idea, they think they should have come up with it. I'd take any offer to manufacture the shoe that would make it worthwhile for me. I've thought about manufacturing and selling it myself. My health is not that great. I could probably make it, but it would kill me in a few years.

False Moves

When Frank S. was 50, in 1972, he gave up a $45,000-a-year job in New York as national sales manager for a large information systems company. He had been there ten years, and the top brass urged him to stay. But his work had changed, and he no longer liked his job. His wife came from Boston, and he found what seemed like a very good job in the area. Nine months after he relocated, his new employer went out of business, and Frank's career has faltered ever since.

Good positions in sales were scarce even for people in their 40s when he started looking in the Boston area, he told us. So he took whatever he could find. All his offers came through ads, and none of the jobs lasted. Either the company collapsed, or the position turned out to be untenable. The longest and highest paid was a $25,000-a-year job that he held for two years when he was in his mid-50s.

A long period of unemployment followed. Finally Frank switched to the nonprofit field, to manage sales and marketing for a workshop for the handicapped.

> The job was terrific. So was my boss. But it paid only $12,000. The boss promised me a raise at the end of a year, and he did try hard, but he couldn't get it for me. So I had to quit.

During the past few years, Frank S. has had one short-term job with a for-profit firm, and a $21,000 position for one year with another handicapped workshop. When we talked, he was applying for an opening outside sales and marketing as a microcomputer manager for a human service agency. "I don't have any achievements in that field, but I could do the job. At 64, I doubt I'll get it."

Old-Fashioned Virtues

"You have different titles but you're basically a salesperson," Ernest K. explained when we talked about his past as a salesman of medical supplies for a large company.

> I never worried about hitting a career plateau like my kids do. You go with a company, you die with a company. I got that mentality from my parents. Then, all of a sudden, you're in your 40s, paddling a canoe without a paddle. You have no specific skills, no real profession. Ten years go by. You're 50. No one wants to bother with you. My age is a prison.

Ernest left after twenty years, when he was 40, because they wanted him to become an administrator. "I didn't want to work in management. I wanted to stay in sales." He could not find another job selling medical supplies, so he started his own business. "Disaster," he said.

Then he held a series of five sales jobs in various fields, all obtained through a headhunter.

> Unemployment was very high. It takes a lot out of you to talk your way into five companies. You're 47, 48. Come for an interview. The guy thinks, what's his problem? He stayed with one company too long. But if you move around, they think you move around too much.

His last job, in insurance, was "the pits. Selling multiple policies to those who could least afford them."

The only work he really enjoyed in all those years was volunteering for his community. "Volunteer work filled a void," he said. He worked four or five nights a week for months, developing a recreation program for his town, took graduate courses in recreation management so that he could choose personnel more effectively. He also chaired local senior citizen committees. "I like helping others. I felt that way when I worked in industry. I didn't want just money."

When we last spoke to him, Ernest was 55 and had given up looking for a full-time job in sales. He had started working a few days a week for a friend who owns a local retail store.

> He pays me $70 a day, which is more than fair of him. I like the work, but there's not enough for me to do sometimes. I hope to expand my role, make a deal that would be very good for both of us. I haven't discussed it with him yet. He's very cautious.

The Happy Bagger

Four years ago Roger A. lost his $29,000-a-year job when the shipyard he worked for, because of the worldwide decline of the shipping industry, reduced its work force. He was 58, had a law degree and years of management experience in labor relations, cost estimating, cost engineering, proposal writing. He spent most of his career with two shipbuilding companies, an industry now on the downward slope.

When unemployment first hit,

> I went to an employment agency the company had recommended. I kept calling them. They never called

back. I answered ads. "We like your resume." Nothing else. I'd have taken a cut in salary, but they don't want to offer you that. You do get discouraged. Lazy, too. I tapered off on looking, took a little law work (wills and estates, title searches), read Plato and other books you thought you wouldn't understand when you were young.

Did his age turn employers off?

I'd rather not say. I'm not sure. Perhaps some of the problem was my health. It was fine, but they ask you at interviews and on forms if you've been in the hospital any time during the last five years. I had been. A very serious operation saved my life.

State law prohibits such questions, we said. "Maybe now, but not then, when I was looking."
Roger's hopes rose when the general employment picture brightened in 1984.

But now there was a Catch-22. Interviewers would ask me, how come you haven't been working? My psyche changed as time went by. I started thinking, I've worked long enough.

He stopped looking for professional work. When we last talked with him, he was bagging groceries twenty-five hours a week in a local supermarket.

Life is sweet. The job keeps me in shape, weight down, waistline down, blood pressure down. You meet nice people. I have a partial pension, an adoring wife, own my house and car, made some good investments. Five kids have graduated from college, the sixth will soon.
I'd take a good offer that came along. I should have gone in for volunteer work to keep continuity. But I'm

happy about life. That operation was a close call. Now when I wake up each morning, it's a beautiful day. I'm grateful. How many good days will I have?

Macro and Micro Causes

The labor market was and is unfriendly to mid-level jobseekers, downright hostile to those over 50. In the for-profit sector, where all the men in this chapter had originally worked and some continued to look, companies were reorganizing or cutting costs or, in manufacturing, cutting back or closing down altogether. Along with so many other workers in declining industries, some of our interviewees were bound to lose the fight for re-entry.

Typically, they hurt themselves with easily made mistakes. Men with backgrounds in manufacturing continued to look only in their field, although intellectually they knew it was shrinking. Others tried too long, as they admitted, to replicate their former high-paid, high-level positions. One man left a solid company at age 50 and relocated with a company he knew very little about. Another clung to sales and marketing, despite discomfort with it that had started before he was 50. He had done well in unpaid community work and enjoyed it, but he had never considered shifting to the public service field.

Like the men and women in the following chapters, some had reached a turning point at the time our last snapshots were taken. Things may have changed for many of them. So our final chapters are not necessarily theirs.

7 | DOWN BUT NOT OUT

The difference between no job and any job is the difference between being a nobody and a somebody, as one job seeker put it. To achieve the transformation, many older workers must not only lower their sights as far as earnings are concerned but also make up their minds to leave their chosen field. Those of our interviewees who made this difficult decision took the step down in order to gain, or preserve, the security of regular salaried employment.

It was a hard choice. The men and women to whom it ultimately brought job satisfaction are distinguished by a high degree of adaptability and optimism. They transformed a traumatic experience into a personal victory.

Reading the Handwriting on the Wall

Millard T. took two years to assess his financial situation and his prospects before deciding to retire at age

58. He was earning $28,000 as production manager of a university publications department where he had been employed for sixteen years. He felt that the pressure on him as a black and as an older person was building up to the point where the stress was almost intolerable.

It became very difficult for me to work. I felt I had to double my show, put out more. The mole on my face became a blemish, while on others it was a beauty spot. My mistakes became glaring. I started going to work Sunday nights, and I was driving thirty-one miles to get there. When you get to be 55 plus you are a little less than secure because everywhere somebody is talking about when are you going to retire, and you see it happening all around you.

Millard is a printer by trade, with thirty-five years of experience. He started as an apprentice at the age of 14 and studied at a technical school of printing. His job was buying printing equipment for the university and for other members of a consortium of higher education institutions.

It was partly his minority status, partly the fact that he was working in an academic environment without a degree, but "basically it was age ideology" that made others anxious to see him gone, he thinks. "Younger people want to see things happen quickly, they think you are a stumbling block, a threat."

One of the experiences that shook him occurred when the decision was made to renovate a building to house electronic typesetting equipment.

At the first staff meeting all they said was let's go with it. All you had to say was "let's consider this technically." No, they didn't want caution from an older person. I gave them all the plans and the feasibility studies, but they didn't show me anything. They

went ahead and spent $25,000 to remodel the build-
ing, but they forgot about the burden circuitry and did
nothing about the air conditioning. Consequently, the
first summer we had a chip meltdown.

That threw me. The thing that really hurt was that
I was the technical person, and none of the people I
had to be responsible to was up to my level of technical knowledge.

Millard also observed the decline of two older white
friends, maneuvered out of jobs when their department
was reorganized while they were absent—one on sab-
batical, the other for an operation. They returned to find
themselves relegated to nondescript functions while
younger managers ran their departments. One had a
nervous breakdown. Other older acquaintances in the
high tech field were offered "promotions" in the form of
transfers abroad—"goodbye, or hello in another
place"—which management knew they were unlikely to
accept.

I think I was lucky in that my expectations were
not very high. You have white, work-ethic, macho men
and this kind of thing happens to them and it just
devastates them. I didn't come with that bag, so I was
able to pack up my little shopping bag and go along.

I had every confidence I was going to find something. I've been on my own since I was 14. I have office
skills. I know cooking. I can estimate.

He had also worked for the Office of Equal Opportunity
and other poverty programs in the 1960s, organizing for
the Job Corps and setting up youth services in various
New England communities.

It did not take Millard long to line up a part-time
post as job counselor with an older workers' employment project, replacing a friend who retired. The pro-

gram's goal is to identify and reduce barriers to jobs facing older, especially minority, unemployed workers.

"I love this work. I'm never going to retire," says Millard. He earns far less than he was getting when he retired. But he has a partial pension, and he and his wife can manage. The mortgage is paid off and their children are grown.

Prove You're Worth More

Nicholas O. was an electrical engineer who had his own manufacturing and consulting firm for 20 years. He has become a recognized expert on employment programs for older professionals, thanks to his willingness to close the door on the past. More than a decade ago, when he was in his mid-50s, with an income of $100,000, he suffered a heart attack that put him in the hospital for several months. While he was recovering, he sent out 400 letters to clients and former business associates explaining that he was forced by illness to take a protracted holiday, but that he hoped he could count on their interest in the future.

> I was testing the climate to see if there was support for rebuilding the business. Not a single person answered. I thought, that's either a commentary on me as a person or on the fact that I've grown old to the point where people don't think there's any value in encouraging me to go back to work.
>
> It was a painful experience, and I decided I had to get out of the business I was in. I volunteered to be the director of a service for unemployed professionals that people in my field had organized. It was up to me to develop and put on workshops for highly skilled people who couldn't find jobs. You got no pay. The rules were that you couldn't stay in the post for more than a year. The point was to get yourself a job as well.

So I went out to look for a job—not in engineering, mind you—a career change. I had a lot of problems with my age, being told that I was overqualified; and finally I had to settle for a job with the state.

The position was located in the city where he lived and involved job development and placement for low-income older people.

I finally convinced them to transfer me to the city payroll. It was an uphill battle, and I can't even describe the horror of the feeling that you somehow can't get hired in a useful job. I eventually moved back to state government to design older worker employment programs. That lasted until federal funding stopped in 1982.

I went to apply for a new position—the same work I had been doing four or five years—the interviewer told me that I didn't have the financial background for the job—this when I had been treasurer of my own business for seven years. The person who eventually got it was a young woman in her 20s.

I put up such a fuss about not being rehired that I was transferred to another state office. They really needed someone who had my skills, so it was a good move for them as well as for me. I felt very lucky, although I wasn't earning a fifth of what I made when I was in business.

Based on his extensive experience working in employment programs for people over 55, the best advice he could give was: Take what you can get.

We have older doctors who come to state job counselors, we have lawyers. We usually get them into jobs. But one thing is certain: No one is going to go back at the pay they were getting before. That's a fact of life. Employers are being very magnanimous and saying they're going to hire older workers, but in fact they are looking to fill entry-level jobs. Our big problem is convincing people that the best way to work is from a position of power. In other words, take the job and prove that you're worth more.

Nicholas followed his own advice cliché. After some five years on the job, he felt that much more could be done for older professional workers who still wanted a career, and that his suggestions for a more aggressive policy on their behalf were not being heard. At that point he answered an ad and retired from state service. At 66, he started a new career as consultant under contract to the government of a small but forward-looking industrial city that he thinks has a chance of becoming a pacesetter in the development of programs to place mature salaried workers. He has put his own experience with age discrimination to work for the public good.

The Long Shadow of the Past

For many, it takes time to rebuild self-confidence after the trauma of a long job search. Raymond V. is happy but nervous. He recently started work in construction purchasing after 20 years in the retail field. Leaving his former occupation did not upset him. His chief worry is that his new boss will catch on to the fact that he is 57 (even though he dyes his hair), and whether it will matter.

They knew I knew nothing about construction when they hired me. I answered an ad and they took me on. Age never came up. The interviewer was a little older than I. The other places, I was interviewed by young ladies in their 20s or 30s. A fellow 40 or 50 didn't have a chance.

Raymond was prepared to take anything to regain a place as a wageworker.

> I'd get up very early, go downtown to Government Center, sit there, look at the paper, get coffee for 30 cents in the cafeteria, make calls from the pay phones. It's comfortable, clean, quiet, no one throws you out. I'd do that for one or two hours, trying to set up appointments. After hunting all day, I put in three or four hours at night, soliciting customers for a long-distance phone company for $5.79 an hour.
>
> I was a grouch to my family, depressed inside all the time. You were taught you were the breadwinner. Now my wife had to support me. You feel like you're nothing, a worm. I'd come home, do the housework. I've got a house to maintain, one of the four kids is still in school.

He expects to make $20,000–25,000 a year in his present position—by putting in a lot of overtime. He has no pension, but is covered by his wife's health benefits— a saving to the company that he thinks is a point in his favor.

> I feel comfortable in this job. My supervisor has told me twice, we're very satisfied with your performance. But I still feel frightened, watch my Ps and Qs. If they tell you, go to lunch at 12:00, be back at 12:30, that's what I do. I'm hoping for the best, that nothing like age catches up with me. Enough is enough.

A Small Lie for a Small Job

Louis P. is one of those for whom "take anything" has meant a step down from a salaried position to an hourly wage, bringing his earnings to less than half of what they were in 1980. Even so, he took ten years off his age to land his present position with a retail chain at $6 an hour.

"I tell people I'm 52. I look younger than I am, and I've cut ten years off my resume. They'll never find out." Experience tells him he would never have gotten the job otherwise.

Louis was 57, and earning $30,000 as district sales manager for the food manufacturing operation of a multinational company, when he was "offered" early retirement in a reduction that affected 350 people. "I loved that job. I hated to leave." He tried being a food broker himself for four years, but "I took a bath. Too much competition from the big companies."

After scouring the food industry vainly for office management jobs, he gave up his old line of work. His memories from fifteen months of job hunting included many short stints in the $5-an-hour bracket, from security guard to clerical worker. So he was gratified when he was taken on as customs clerk for an export–import broker, though the pay was only $300 a week. Louis had majored in international trade in college, so he felt he was qualified. He soon noticed he was doing twice as much work as anyone else.

The owner was around 40. He liked me, and he used to call me into his office just to chat. One day he asked me how old I was. I told him I was 60. He turned around, muttered something. I said, "What?" He said, "Anything wrong with your hearing?" I went back to work. Half an hour later he asks if I'm feeling all right. I say fine. Every hour he puts this question. "Lou," he says, "there's a box of sand in the warehouse. Put some sand on the steps, they're icey."

He had a gofer to do those things, but I wasn't going to knuckle under and I did it. Fourth day he calls me in. "Lou," he says, "I made a mistake. I don't have enough work. Come part time." I said OK. The next day my immediate boss told me to do something with the file system. It was impossible without instruction. Sally will show you. She gave me one minute. I quit.

When you're young you're a member of society, one of us. When you're more mature you stand out, you're different, people feel uncomfortable. I've found out what it's like to be black.

Race, Gender—and Age

Ethel C., 60, is black and she finds age a heavier burden than color or gender. "You learn to live with and do something about being black and female. Over 55 is devastating if you're not well entrenched."

Ethel worked as a paraprofessional in social work and mental health for church and community groups during the 1960s and 1970s, first in Boston and then in Delaware. When funding began to dry up, she started her own catering business.

I enjoyed it, and it kept a roof over my head. But in 1983 I gave it up to come back to Boston and help take care of a grandchild. Then I just couldn't seem to find a job. I had two years of only sketchy employment, but I never collected unemployment insurance because they made you feel like you were on welfare, asking for a handout.

She tried to return to the human services field.

I wasn't looking for great money. I answered an ad for low-income people offering training as a nurse's assistant or medical secretary. I thought I could handle it, so I went in and took the test. I was interviewed by a man who asked me, "What about arthritis?" I said, "What about it?" I was never accepted. I questioned other women who were there, but none of them were asked anything like that. One of them said, his job is coming up for evaluation and he's afraid you might get it.

Ethel's daughter saw a story in the paper about a voluntary agency serving low-income older workers, and Ethel went in for an interview. Although the human services were beginning to revive, the agency dealt only with for-profit employers. They sent her to a company that is willing to hire over-55s in entry-level positions. Ethel was taken on as a clerk, first as a temporary, then as a permanent employee at $11,000. She hopes to get a chance to move up.

> We're paid at poverty rates. I made more as a para-professional years ago. But they train you, and this is a step forward for me right now. It pays some of the bills, and I feel better about myself just getting up and going to work every morning.

Employers who have made the decision to hire older workers find it in their own interest to improve the working atmosphere for them, as Ethel has observed.

> Here we're all ages and we're on a first-name basis, We got a new manager recently, a dynamic woman in her 30s. I went to see her and said I'd transfer out if my age mattered. I'd been thinking about it because the former manager who had been there fifteen, sixteen years, was chauvinistic, surrounded himself with young girls. He had a subtle, laid-back way of making you feel insignificant. I thought I'd better get out before I blew up, but the new manager saw this, and she asked me not to.
> The company is getting very strict about how people conduct themselves. They won't tolerate discrimination. Lots of older people are being hired. Our problem, older people's problem, is that they get to believe the myths: that we can't do anything, can't

learn anything. Losing faith in yourself is the cruelest
thing that can happen to you.

The Risk-Taker

A man who has set out to prove that he belongs at the
top is Kenneth F., 63 and doing manual labor as a construction worker on a condominium development project about forty miles from his home. He has twenty
years behind him as a college football coach, has written books, done part-time teaching. Most recently he
worked as a purchasing agent but had been laid off four
years before we interviewed him, when the company
was sold. He receives a small pension from the Veterans'
Administration; none from any of his jobs. His aim was
to find an administrative position or get back into
coaching. But after "floundering around" for two years,
he took a job as a laborer with a construction company
at $7 an hour.

> No benefits, forty hours a week. I moved up to
> carpenter a month later but no pay increase. The
> owner called me at 5:30 one morning, in trouble. I
> helped him. Then I told him I wanted to be supervisor.
> Now I'm making $11 an hour as crew supervisor with
> twenty men under me.
> I lug lumber all day. I enjoy work, now more than
> ever. You have to grow, go on learning. This is a very
> exciting time of my life if I can put it together. I'm a
> fighter. I don't sit back and let people walk all over me.
> If something bad happens, I don't cry or sulk, I just
> leave.
> I get up at 4:30 A.M. I'm on the job at 7:30, leave by
> 3:30. I've lost fifty pounds since I started this job. I feel
> excellent, and everyone who knows me says I look ten
> years younger. But when I come home I'm exhausted,
> just crawl into bed.

People come to me for advice. I do all the planning on procurement for the job. I've told them I want to be boss of the new project they're starting, and they said they'd consider it. If I don't get it, I'll leave. I have no idea what I'll do, but I feel that if someone can use me, appreciate my talents, that's everything.

The Wrong Change or the Wrong Time

Older workers cannot afford to make capricious career changes as Lillian R. discovered when she tried to break into academic life in her late 50s. She did not realize that years of experience and publication precede a permanent appointment, and that the competition for tenured positions leaves many promising young scholars in temporary and part-time jobs, if not unemployed.

I was the first in my family to go to college. We are talking about an individual who didn't have any relatives in academia, who didn't know anybody in academia, and didn't know what was involved. I was just dumb and confident.

Lillian had started as an elementary school teacher. As a young woman she followed a familiar interrupted work-life pattern, moving from city to city as her husband changed jobs.

The first year anywhere I'd be a mother, and the second year I'd get a job. The result of this start–stop kind of thing is that today all my teaching jobs would entitle me to a Social Security of $350 a month. It makes you bitter.

She abandoned school teaching when she was 50 because she found herself in "an extremely difficult situation."

I had left the nice upper-class elementary school where I had tenure partly because of frustration at the lack of innovation, and partly out of a sense of *noblesse oblige*. And I went with several friends to teach at a boarding school for urban welfare children. I was not accredited, not everyone on the staff was qualified, and it was bedlam, it was a zoo. Middle-class values were on a collision course with reality.

After taking a year off to take care of an older relative, Lillian went to work part time at a small community college.

The minute I walked onto that campus I had this feeling of coming home, and I knew I wanted to get into the academic world. I enrolled at a state university in the sociology department and got a fellowship. At our very first interview the department chair said, you know I can't promise you a job. But I was thinking less about what I was going to do than about being a student.

Like many women who married during or shortly after the Second World War and violated the accepted norm for wives and mothers by remaining in the paid work force, Lillian's jobs were usually short-term compromises between her interests and family needs. Ability to improvise was more important than planning ahead. Lillian did not think like a career woman.

By the time she had her degree, she had decided to separate from her husband; and she moved to Boston to be near one of her daughters. Through new acquaintances she got a job with a professional organization, and that led to teaching at a university during the summer session. For the next two years, she subsisted on one-semester appointments, teaching one or two courses—no health benefits, no teachers' retirement plan.

Part-time teaching is very exploitative. And we are a threat to full-time teachers, so they aren't very sympathetic. Sociology wasn't a thriving field, and there were plenty of candidates for every opening. At the same time, I have to admit that I wasn't very energetic, and I wasn't very knowledgeable, and I wasn't very smart. I'm a good teacher and I enjoy teaching and get good evaluations, but I was 59 when I got my degree, and the pattern of my life was set. I didn't go out and do the research and writing that prove you are a professional.

Unlike Nicholas O., Raymond V., Louis P., and Kenneth F., who have working wives to back them up, and in common with Ethel C., Lillian has to depend entirely on herself for her present and future income. She has only a small teacher's pension.

Two years ago I bit the bullet and told my chairman I couldn't live like that any more. He was always looking for courses I could teach, but I told him I had to get a job I could count on, one with health benefits. I had worked as a secretary at one of the universities when I first came to Boston, and I knew I wanted to be there. After one false start, I found a place, and that's where I am today.

I had a hard time of it at first. I work for four professors. Three of them were all for me, but the fourth, who was the youngest and the fiercest, was ready to fire me because my turn-around time wasn't fast enough.

He thought I was too old for the job. He didn't say that, of course. He said things like "Well, I understand these computers, but I realize that your generation . . ." He set everyone's mind against me, and when evaluation time came around I got a bad one. But I had no alternative. At the next performance review I got rave notices from everyone.

As for my former severest critic, I've turned his life around. He's a very anxious person. But I'm so well organized that I give him a good foundation, and he thinks I'm wonderful. Yes, I like the job now. I've just been upped to $17,000. It's not great and it's not what I'd be getting if I'd stayed in elementary school teaching—I'd be making about $30,000 by now—but it's got benefits, holidays, access to credit.

Lillian took a big step down when there was no alternative. She was 65 when we last spoke with her, and planned to stay in her secretarial job a few more years to improve her Social Security prospects.

"My case shows something about people's mindsets," she says.

I had no socialization in the academic world. I could have gone back and got certified as an elementary school teacher in Massachusetts, but it would have been difficult to get a job. With my experience, I was too expensive. Yet because in the past I'd got everything I did get on my own, and I'd been pretty good at working within the system, I assumed it would always be like that. That's why it was so disturbing to find out that at my age the system isn't where it used to be for me.

The system is not there for most people over 50 who lose a job or want a career change. Those who succeed, do so by making the most of limited chances.

Free-lancing has been a successful strategy for many trying to evade the age barrier, as we will see in the next chapter.

8 | HALF A LOAF

All of our job losers wanted full-time employment at close to the same salary and level of responsibility as their last long-term position, preferably in the same line of work. They did not want the more leisurely pace of part-time employment that older workers are said to yearn for. But, for the majority, getting it all turned out to be impossible. As we saw in the last chapter, some gave priority to the security of a permanent job. To find it, they entered fields remote from their original occupation and accepted sizeable reductions in income.

Another substantial minority discovered, some much sooner than others, that holding out for full-time salaried employment wasn't worth the wait or the bad odds, when most available full-time work was in non-professional jobs at low hourly wages. They refused to slide down the ladder they had spent years climbing. As life without work became increasingly unbearable—financially, psychologically, or both—they chose one of two other routes to get back to work.

Most went into short-term, temporary employment as contract workers or consultants. A few took full-time sales positions, with earnings based on commission. Neither arrangement provides regular paychecks, benefits, or job security. But both choices offered the chance to use their professional, management, or technical skills rather than settle for the safety of regular but less challenging work.

The Temporary May Be Permanent

Those who sought short-term employment, whether through agencies or by setting up on their own, joined a fast growing corps of professionals and managers in temporary jobs throughout the country. More employers are using mid-to-high-level temporary workers than ever before, according to 1986 reports in business journals. Secretaries, nurses, writers, commercial artists, and other specialists have free-lanced for years, and business consultants are nothing new. Why the flurry of interest?

The extent and variety of the demand for "top drawer temps," as *Time Magazine* has dubbed them, has never been so widespread. Employing institutions, large and small, are hiring short-term accountants, chief executive and financial officers, doctors, engineers, lawyers, marketing and public relations experts, programmers, technical writers, and dozens of other professionals. New agencies have sprung up to provide them, and long-established temporary employment services have added new personnel categories.

The boom may be temporary, but some labor market experts predict that it is the wave of the future. They expect corporations to continue cutting permanent positions, and to expand their use of temporary workers to perform the middle-level tasks that still need doing, at far less cost. The employer finds a qualified person for a particular project, lets them go when the job is done or even earlier. No need to carry someone on the payroll during slack periods or, as the *Wall Street Journal* put it, "stick with a lemon." Temporaries get none of the benefits that now amount to 40 percent or more of many employers' payrolls.

What employers gain—short-term workers lose. Although their hourly pay is usually higher than a permanent employee's, payless periods between jobs can last weeks or months. No benefits means no paid holidays, vacations, sick leave, health insurance or pension. As these situations succeed, they create a Catch-22: Employers who use short-term professionals may be inspired to make even more cuts in mid-level jobs than originally planned because temporary workers prove so cost-effective.

On the other hand, if part-time professionalism becomes a permanent fixture in the American workplace, it may offer the best comeback opportunity for older job seekers. For them the challenge is to make the best of the opportunities and find ways of dealing with the disadvantages.

Access Through Employment Agencies

For-profit employment agencies have been handling short-term professional placements in engineering and technical jobs for some time. Frederick H. obtained almost all his contracts from one of those agencies. He had registered with at least eight shortly after he lost his last full-time job, four years before we talked to him. He still calls all of them between temporary engagements, as well as checking in with his most recent employer. He has also joined support groups. At one he listened to other people's problems ("It was helpful"); at another he took an abilities test (also "useful"). How to find temporary work or establish a career as a consultant was never mentioned.

Frederick had been making $22,500 when a mass layoff at his place of work hit him at age 56. Although he has not made that kind of money since, he has done fairly well considering the forces arrayed against him.

He worked for years in the ailing smokestack industries, the last seven in steam combustion, one of the hardest-hit sectors. His professional expertise in mechanical engineering and design is no longer in demand. "Mechanical engineer jobs, forget it," the executive of a large employment agency in the technical field told us. "Computer hardware manufacturers used to hire some, but they're closing down, moving south, getting parts made overseas and just assembling here."

When we first spoke, Frederick had been jobless for four months.

> I've had no interviews in all that time. Over the last twenty-four months I've had sixteen of work. On the last contract I was making $18 an hour. Now I get $200 a week in unemployment.

A few months later, a $600-a-week contract came through in mechanical drafting via the agency that had provided most of his work.

> The project I'll be working on is part of Star Wars. I'd rather have a real job. When large companies take you, they're already six to eight weeks behind, looking for an outsider to do wonders.

Frederick hasn't given up hope of finding full-time, permanent employment, and continues to look.

I'll take anything that's compatible in electrical or
mechanical design, drafting, or project management.
But I won't work in a machine shop at $5 an hour. I
went as far as San Diego and Florida, looking. Discrimination is definitely out there. It's not blatant, I
can't put my finger on it. Believe me, I haven't passed
up any full-time opportunities. I've even gone back to
the drafting board just to get work, something I left
years ago.

Movable Skills

Contract work has restored Donald C.'s pride and
earning power. "I've never been happier," he told us. His
jobs have been in the power industry, seemingly a far
cry from his former work in department store operations management, though his tasks are not dissimilar.
His first short-term situation, two years before we
talked and four years after he lost his last full-time job
at age 58, required establishing receiving procedures
during the repiping of a nuclear power plant. It lasted
eight months.

Several months elapsed before the second contract
materialized and provided four months' work at a nuclear plant in another state.

"I was hired as an expediter but I ended up doing
traffic control. They gave me an excellent reference." A
third offer, on a nonnuclear project, also out-of-state,
came through from the first employer between two of
our interviews. Donald expected it to continue for at
least six months. His wife, a teacher, planned to join
him for the summer.

The source of his good fortune was a no-fee public
agency: the state employment service. "I spent a lot of
time at three different job-match centers run by the
state, going through microfiche for local jobs. I looked at
the out-of-state jobs too. I'll go anywhere they'll send

me." It was at one of the state agencies that he found his first power plant listing, and that one led to the next.

Donald had an unusually grueling job-loss experience (described in Chapter Two), followed by four years of jobs that didn't work out. Contracting has been a welcome contrast. "A wonderful experience, very satisfying. You come in to do a job. They let you do it. They were pleased with what you did. They paid you well."

Despite his enthusiasm Donald, like Frederick H., has not become a full-fledged consultant. When temporary work ends, he continues to answer ads for full-time employment, while he maintains contact with the agency and the company that launched him on a contracting career.

Women's Ways and Means

The women who went into short-term work came closer to adopting the entrepreneurial style than the men we interviewed. Like most women of their age who started at the bottom years ago and rose into management, their field was office work. Getting ahead not only required office skills but also enterprising, improvising abilities to overcome formidable sex barriers.

The promise of a rise from humble beginnings in office work to professional positions continues to be held out by employers and by office-work schools and placement agencies to attract lower level applicants. Learn to type, keep books, and handle a word processor to get your foot in the door. Then work hard and well and the sky's the limit.

The women we interviewed who are now in contract work provide proof both positive and negative of this promise. They ascended the office-work career ladder to well-paid, responsible positions. But when they were in their 40s or early 50s the corporate tide turned against them. That their experience was limited to women's work only, as well as their age, limited their opportunities.

Patricia D. is a prime example. She had been earning $36,000 as a full-charge bookkeeper and business manager for six nursing homes, when the owner sold five to a national chain about two years before our interview. She was then 55, never married, had a college degree, years of experience in accounting, data processing, financial record-keeping, office management.

"I didn't want to go with the buyer, as some of the other employees did. That was a good decision, because he's had a lot of trouble." So she stayed on to manage the remaining nursing home. After a few months of being a one-woman office, she resigned.

"I collected unemployment insurance for the maximum period. Why spoil this once-in-a-lifetime chance not to work? I was in no hurry to look for a job because I was so sure I'd find one, so confident because of my experience."

Then came months of fruitless search, with her age as her major handicap, she believes.

> I tried everything, even went to public accountants to see if they needed a bookkeeper for smaller clients, grunge work where you run the place. They couldn't give me one lead. You suffer from age. I can't believe this is happening to me. It kills me that my record doesn't mean anything. I'm outgoing, easy to talk to, like young people, like change. I'd take a good job at $20,000 and I tell people that.

At the time of our first conversation, Patricia was working on two temporary assignments she had found on her own. "I held out for $12 an hour," she said.

"There's an awful lot of part-time work out there, and age discrimination lessens." Because of what she learned about the temporary market, Patricia seriously considered buying a temporary employment agency she saw advertised for sale. She consulted a free counseling service for small entrepreneurs and was advised against buying.

> The counselor who talked to me had been with a very successful management consulting firm. He explained that it would be 90% selling, 10% consulting. Another counselor there, a woman who had owned and run an employment agency, also advised against it. I prefer working to selling anyway.

The last time we talked, Patricia was waiting to hear about a potential full-time job in office management. "It pays $18,000, but it's worth much more and so am I. It's an insult. And it's an eighteen mile drive each way, but I may take it. I have to support myself."

The Long Road Back

Helen B. and Patricia D. have a lot in common. Both went to work full time in the clerical field at an early age. Both progressed far in terms of what women could expect to achieve. Both tumbled when the company they worked for changed hands.

A young executive of the shoe company where Helen worked spotted her in the steno pool when she was 20 and asked her to become his assistant. She stayed with him for twenty-three years. As he rose to the top to become president of the company, she rose with him. By 1975, at 43, she was a member of the corporate planning committee and the highest paid female employee in the company, making $25,000 plus a $5,000 bonus.

The company was taken over in a hostile raid. "I stayed where I was for two years. In 1977 the new owners decided to close the office, and I didn't want to relocate." Today Helen, 54, supports herself as an independent contractor in word processing and administrative work at $15 an hour.

The first job she took after leaving the shoe company when she was 45 paid $22,000 with no bonus.

> I was supposed to be executive assistant to a CEO-chairman of the board, and I was sure I could work my way up where I had been in no time. The job turned out to be very different from its title. He wanted a personal assistant, not an executive assistant, someone to water his plants at home and wait for furniture deliveries.

Helen left after two years to go into business on her own, entering a new field (as Patricia D. had considered doing). She sold real estate, taking temporary clerical jobs to supplement her income. Like Patricia, she didn't like selling.

> I had difficulty convincing someone to plunk their life savings into a house when I wasn't really convinced they should. I'd be able to sell a product, but not such a huge commitment.

After two years she went looking again for full-time employment in order to support herself and her mother. Through an ad she found a job as administrator at a hospital. She was paid out of government grants that began to dwindle. So she located another job, this time as assistant to the president of a small consulting firm. It all but went under eighteen months later.

I was on unemployment most of 1984. I answered ads, went to a counseling agency, to employment agencies, networked with people I knew, people they knew. I got lots of interviews, sometimes five or six at the same company. I was looking for an administrative type position. I didn't care whether it was at the top corporate level. Often I was one of two or three finalists, but I never got the job. I even went to a commercial career agency that charged $2000 for doing nothing.

Age barriers in the full-time market forced Helen into contract work.

One agency I visited said that a certain company was one of the few that doesn't talk too much about wanting younger applicants, but they always seem to hire them. Several told me a job came in, we told them about you, they said we're looking for someone younger.

People would bring it up at job interviews. "At one I was asked, 'I know this is illegal but how would you get along with younger people? You'd be the oldest person in the office.'" She found contract work altogether different.

A place where I had interviewed for a permanent job and got the usual thanks-but-no-thanks letter called me for a spot job as a contractor two months later. I worked there six to eight weeks, had dealings with the person they had hired for the job I was interviewed for. She was about 26 and had very little experience. A while later they offered me four to six months, five days a week. I refused. I didn't especially like the company or the work, and I didn't want to lose my other clients.

Helen was doing well when we spoke. Her clients come to her through acquaintances and word of mouth.

> I'm sometimes too busy to take someone, and I lose them. Some jobs are one day a week for several weeks, some a week or two to fill in for vacations. A law firm would like a longer commitment from me, but I won't take it. I already lost clients because I work for that firm two days a week.

Why not build up what you've started, and hire someone so you can take on more clients, we asked. "I don't want to make the investment of money and time," she replied. "I'd like to retire at 65, eleven years from now, and I need to build up my reserves." Helen is still looking for a permanent full-time job, getting interviews but no offers.

On Contract to a Contractor

Helen B. and other short-term workers might jump at the chance to make arrangements like Gene W.'s. He works one-half to three-quarters time for an engineering consultant firm, and doesn't have to sell himself to get assignments and keep them flowing. The head of the business does that, a man who once worked for Gene.

> We had a good relationship. I found him again through a relative when I was job hunting, and he was just about to go into business. He needed experts he could offer to clients, so he was glad to hear from me. He marks me up double when he places me. I'm actually making more per hour than when I had a full-time position, but no benefits.

Gene had been forced into early retirement about eighteen months earlier when he was 55. A division manager in a construction company, he was earning $50,000 a year after twenty years of service. He rejected early retirement offers until he was told that his division was to be merged and there would be no place for him after reorganization.

Like most interviewees, he thought he would find another job right away. But the ads he answered didn't produce offers, nor did the resumes he sent out. He has learned, like others before him, that age is less of a barrier in consulting. Corporations want seasoned, experienced, professionals in this role.

Although he doesn't have to hustle for business and he makes good money, consulting has a serious drawback for Gene: too much travel. So he is answering ads again for a full-time job, and when we last talked was being "actively considered for two."

Short-term Worker's Dream

Norris J. never looked for short-term work; it came to him unsolicited from his former employer, a utilities company. He was 62, working in a low-level, full-time job when he grabbed the offer to set up and run a computerized operation. He was still a contract worker for the company eighteen months later when we last spoke to him. He is included here because he got what many older job seekers want: another chance with a former employer. His case is unique among our interviewees.

The prototype of the faithful employee, Norris had worked for the state subsidiary of a large public utility for thirty-eight years. The breakup of the company also broke up his career.

I was making $40,000 plus as foreman-supervisor in the engineering department. My job went south in 1983, and I didn't want to move. My home, my family, my life is here in New England. I got a transfer to another department up here at the same salary, but I didn't really like it.

Early retirement offers came his way early in 1984 when he was 62.

You didn't have to accept it, but you'd be taking a chance if you didn't. The younger people wanted to get rid of us. They were worried about their jobs. I had seniority like the union members do. That was company policy, but you could tell how the younger ones felt. They'd say it once in a while in a joking way; you felt the barbs. I left in June.

After several weeks at home, fixing things around the house, "I couldn't stand it. I was vegetating. I've got to be in the world. I love fixing things as a hobby, but that's all."

He looked for work through a nonprofit employment agency.

"I went through the book of leads from companies wanting older people. The salaries were ridiculous, $4.75 an hour. I'm old, but I still have talent." He didn't contact his old employer. "I knew they didn't want me around." Nor did he ask friends, relatives, former colleagues. "They knew I was looking. I wasn't destitute."

After several weeks of dead-end interviews, he took a job as a janitor, full-time, at $7.50 an hour. "They offered it as part-time because they thought that was what I wanted. I said no, I want to work 40 hours a week, as I always have. I was there a few weeks when the company called and offered me a better type of work at $11 an hour."

When the first contract ended, another was offered immediately and Norris grabbed that too. Everything had gone well until shortly before our conversation.

They're on an economy kick, still in the red. They want me to take $8 instead of $11. Could be that I'll be out again. I'm worried. Even if I am old, I need something to do with enough money to make it worth my while. I like to be a member of the work force, get up in the morning and go in, close my desk, so to speak, at five.

I've never forgotten the motto over the entrance at my high school: Work is one of our greatest blessings. Everyone should have an occupation.

Commission Sales: Two Paths

Working on commission can be very satisfying. You are your own boss most of the time, meet lots of people, make lots of money. A drawing account from your employer tides you over dry periods. Lack of benefits is offset by income tax deductions for your car, home telephone and other business-related expenses. Most important, your hard work and creative skills put money in your pocket, not just the company's. Or so you are asked to believe.

All this is true for some people some of the time, but many more try than succeed in earning a decent living in commission sales. The product or service to be sold may be shoddy and unmarketable. The competition may be cut-throat. The work may require skills that the salesperson does not have or want to develop. Drawing accounts must be replenished. Tax deductions may be much lower than the cost of having no paid leave or health coverage.

Among our older job losers, selling on commission, whether as a company employee with earnings based entirely on sales, or as a sales representative working under contract, was not a popular alternative to a regular job. A handful of men did well at it; only two women tried commission work at all. One of them,

Helen B., disliked and abandoned it as we have seen. The other, Margery S. became Massachusetts sales representative for a children's book publisher, and was still at it when we talked a year later.

Sales representatives, in contrast to employees working on commission, must provide their own office space, telephone, and secretarial services. Although they can deduct these and other expenses from their taxes eventually, they must pay the bills first. There is no drawing account with the company to help the cash flow. Many companies require that the prospective salesperson pay anywhere from a few hundred to several thousand dollars to purchase the merchandise to be sold before obtaining the sales representative designation. After that sales reps must replenish their stocks and meet other costs, so they are often out of pocket.

Commission selling follows gender lines. Until recently, women employed on commission worked only in a few retailing areas: women's designer clothes, residential real estate, and a few other products and services that women "understand." Men sold a wide variety of wares with a much bigger profit potential: household appliances and other "big ticket" items; commercial real estate; stocks and securities; insurance; and industrial and commercial products, equipment, and services.

The title of sales representative belonged almost wholly to men until a few years ago, when women began to be recruited for an expanding sideline: direct sales to women in their own home or at demonstration "parties" in the homes of friends or neighbors. The products are those women buy, and are relatively inexpensive: handicraft kits, Tupperware, cosmetics, crystal, china, educational toys. Commissions are predictably modest.

Uphill but Upbeat

Margery S. is one of these women, selling a line of children's books house-to-house. She made $17,000 in commissions her first year, before expenses. To make that much she works hard, seven days a week.

My car costs are high, and my volume is lower than average, but I have the highest sales closing rate, and the company vp in New York loves me. He's about 30.

She has other sources of income, but earning money is essential to her self-esteem. "It makes me independent. I could never not have my own money, my own bank account. When I was young I felt guilty if I spent on myself. Not now, I earn it."

Visits to schools all over the state to demonstrate the books and gain access to prospective customers—the parents of students—is the first stage in her campaign. Then she visits the parents' homes, a dozen or more a week, mostly at night. "I have to find houses in all kinds of areas. Sometimes I start home at 11 P.M. But I'd rather sleep in my own bed than spend the night—and the money—in a motel."

Margery had looked for salaried jobs after she left private school teaching at age 61, when "they fired the principal and the new headmistress said she wanted young, progressive thinkers." Rather than compete with the many young people looking for teaching jobs, she applied for positions outside education in fields where she thought her teaching skills and experience would count. Although she shaved a few years off her resume, age could not be disguised, she discovered, when she appeared in person. "One interviewer asked if I was a grandmother, several inquired about my health."

After she went into direct sales she continued to answer ads for salaried jobs. One sounded just right, selling a reading system at $17,000 plus commission.

> The job called for experience in sales and teaching, and I had both. They asked, "Do you think you have the energy? There's a lot of travel. You'll hear from us." I did. They said my qualifications didn't quite fit.
>
> I tried to see the head of the company by applying again when they repeated the ad. I made friends with the secretary and asked about who'd been hired so far. All young, she told me, with not much experience. What about teaching? Oh, she said, we put that in our ad so we won't get illiterate applicants.

Margery has also ventured into acting, and sees that as a future source of income. Several years ago she noticed an ad for extras for a television serial to be filmed in Boston, and sent in her resume.

> I never heard, and forgot all about it. A few months ago I got a call the day before they wanted me to appear. I went. It was an outdoor shot in the rain and the cold, but I loved every second. I got another call in three weeks; an interior scene and that was a lot warmer. A third call came when I was abroad, so I missed that job.

One of her six children, an actor, arranged for "head shots," so Margery could apply for work in television commercials.

> I'm going to New York to have them taken. I could play a retiree who's bought land in Florida, loves it, and advises other people to invest. Or maybe say how good Geritol makes me feel. My real avocation has always been the theatre. This is the best time of my life, and I plan to make the most of it.

Technician on Commission

Philip A., 55, works part-time on commission as a certified, registered appraiser at a real estate office, a change of field as well as pace. He assesses his present situation this way: "Things are a lot better for me than they were."

Like Frederick H., Philip had been in mechanical engineering, a declining field, when he lost his last full-time job with a large engineering consulting firm three years earlier. "It was a Saturday night massacre" that eliminated everyone who earned over $25,000, "naturally mostly older workers." His field, and the firm's main thrust, construction engineering, was in deep trouble.

Job hunting for several years produced no offers in Massachusetts or anywhere else. Philip has a heart condition, for which he received a partial disability pension. Since he has come in second in several competitions for jobs, he does not think his health has been a factor. He has amassed plenty of evidence that age alone is a hopeless handicap.

> I was told by people in personnel offices point blank, forget it. The chances of your getting a job in the $35–40K category are remote. Most of us are letting everybody over 50 go.

Philip tried consulting on his own but found he was banging his head against a closed door.

> A lot of people are freelancing in engineering. The architects have their own consultants with whom they've been working for years. They're very polite, put your name on file, say "don't call us we'll call you." Everyone knows what that means.

Instead he took several courses in real estate appraisal to obtain certification.

> I came out with a 95% average, a helluva lot higher than a lot of the younger people. My engineering background lends itself to the work. It's long hours, there's lots of home preparation, and I'm working harder than I did before. But commission work is something to turn to when you're up against age discrimination.

Success, More or Less

Thomas Y. had started his career in commission sales three years before we interviewed him. He had previously spent more than a year searching for an executive job in marketing similar to the one he had lost at 62. He had earned $75,000 as head of a marketing division in a giant consumer products firm.

> I was forced to take early retirement when the company closed the division. They found something for everyone else in it who wanted to stay. I was the oldest. They told me plainly they couldn't use me anywhere else in the company.

He knew his age would be a problem, "but I felt that there might be that one great opportunity out there for someone with my forty years of varied marketing experience, my unusual achievements, and an MBA, if I looked hard enough."

He answered ads, went to headhunters, tried consulting on his own, and then:

> The exact perfect job turned up. A European kitchen appliance manufacturer wanted someone to manage all their U.S. marketing. I had done the same thing on my old job. I fit the requirements so well that

a headhunter promoted me for the position in spite of my age. I was one of four finalists and had an excellent meeting but I didn't get it. The headhunter told me off the record that the company felt I was the best candidate but they felt they needed a more youthful image to build their market.

I realized then that age discrimination was such that I would never get back to where I'd been. So I sat down and figured out what I could do with my experience, and I discovered an occupation for people like me by answering an ad for Executive Sales.

Companies hire people like him for those positions, Thomas explained, "because they have products that must be sold to top level people in top level companies. Not everyone is comfortable doing that. You have to be at home in the executive suite, understand *Fortune* 500 people."

What he sells has nothing to do with any product he marketed before. The large international company that he works for provides energy related services to corporations, and Thomas is a district sales manager.

Resources Needed

Many Americans believe that older people are set in their ways, lack creative and physical energy, resist change, want to stay put. But the men and women we talked to show these beliefs to be nothing but stereotypes. Their driving need to work and unwillingness to take unskilled or semiskilled jobs have propelled them into commission work, whether for a limited time or permanently.

The temporary workers have had to adjust early and often to new work locations, company cultures, bosses, colleagues and tasks. Commission salespeople frequently have to travel, work evenings and long hours, establish rapport with strangers almost every day, handle tasks they had never performed before.

True, they still look back with nostalgia on the life of a permanent, full-time employee, and would envy the men and women in the next chapter who recaptured it. Nevertheless, their capacity to adjust to the change from working for an employer to working on their own deserves support.

The direct sales field, reported the Direct Selling Association (DSA) in 1986, involves close to six million free-lancers, mostly part-timers and women. DSA, a trade organization with 130 member-companies that use direct sales, predicts that more firms will sell products and services directly to consumers in the future. Its members may have openings in your community (1776 K Street, NW, Washington, D.C., 20006).

Although commission work, whether selling to wholesalers and retailers or direct to the customer, is no panacea for older job seekers, the pros and cons should be explored. Assumptions that many people have about being unable or unwilling to do what it takes to sell may be incorrect. A short course in sales techniques is one way to examine the field, and not only through the curriculum. The instructor and some students may have work experience and contacts for additional information.

The cons to beware of include poor quality products, requirements for cash up front, delays in delivery to consumers and payment to salespeople. Talking to people who already sell for the company can produce considerable enlightenment. Reliable firms will offer such opportunities. Of course, they will select people who like what they are doing and not refer you to drop-outs. Nevertheless, a lot can be learned by asking the right questions. In addition to inquiries about the cons mentioned above, information about the pros should also be sought. For example:

How much and what kind of training does the company offer, when and where? Are sales personnel reimbursed for travel and other training-related expenses? What about the reimbursement for telephone calls, gas, other sales-related expenses? What, if any, career ladder is available? What are the average net earnings a month for how many hours of work including time spent making appointments, traveling to them, keeping records?

Temporary and contract agencies, the other major source of mid-level work when full-time employment is not available, should also be screened. Visiting several to observe them at work and to ask about their pay rates, rules, and clients can provide a basis for comparison and choice. What does the agency charge the client for what kinds of jobs, and what does it pay the worker? Are there any paid benefits? Does the agency require an "exclusive" from workers who sign up, or may they register with other agencies?

Nonprofit and public agencies that help older job seekers should help them explore and assess the part-time market. Recommendations appear in Chapter Ten.

9 | WINNERS' CIRCLE

In this chapter we describe some of the interviewees who found (or kept) full-time jobs in their field, at salaries close to what they had been earning in their last ones, or with a reasonably good chance of reaching the same levels. Not all did equally well; but our standard of success was how near they came to their individual goals. Together they show that careers need not be limited by age, that assertive behavior can do more good than harm, that the business world is not the only place to look for jobs, and that acquiring new professional or technical skills pays off.

Those who managed to resume their careers are too few to permit generalizations. Among those who succeeded there is a larger number of women than in our sample as a whole. Among the employers, government and nonprofit organizations are disproportionately represented. These are predictable results, however, considering that most new jobs today are in service fields, which include public and nonprofit employers, and that women are the majority of workers in the service occupations.

What made these particular people "winners"? Most had concrete technical skills that were in demand. But we believe that the dogged determination with which they pursued their goals was decisive.

State of Salvation

Norman D. had always been an accountant. His initial brush with unemployment came in 1972, a recession year, when he was 42. His first serious encounter with the barriers of age occurred in 1980. He was 51 and vice president in charge of finance in a manufacturing company, earning $36,000, when the company was suddenly liquidated.

> I was out of work eighteen months. That's when I began to feel the effects of age. I got no response from anyone. There aren't that many jobs as chief financial comptroller, and you're competing with 30-year-olds with Harvard MBAs.
>
> Business is of the mind-set that young people coming in can grow with the firm. It doesn't happen that way, but that's the psychology. They don't want the 40s or 50s who'll be with them ten years and then get pensions. People don't say it, naturally, But after you've sent out hundreds of resumes, gone to agencies, try every which way, learn about jobs that fit you like a glove, hear nothing, you begin to understand.

Norman's unemployment benefits ran out. He spent all his savings, and financial problems were compounded by family difficulties, ending in divorce. Finally another comptroller's job at $36,000 came along.

He took it, although he realized the firm was shaky, and indeed it lasted only a year.

> Age began to be a real problem. I sent out more resumes than I ever had in my entire life. I was at the end of my rope. Broke. I looked around for any source of help.

Help came from one of the private agencies with programs directed at low-income job seekers over 55. They found him a position as director of fiscal audits with a state office at $27,000. It isn't ideal, but he expects things to improve.

> The pay is low, but the job is new and it isn't graded properly. It will go up. The benefits are only ten percent of what I used to get. But I was literally just staying alive. It was a tough battle. It's in my area of expertise. I'm very busy. I just hope it lasts.

Another refugee from private enterprise who found a second career in government employ is Stanley A. A purchasing agent with a large manufacturer, he lost his job at 39 when the company moved south and he decided not to go with it. Through a friend he located a job almost immediately with an engineering consulting firm, first as an "inside expediter" on a giant construction project, later purchasing supplies for the in-house use of the corporation.

At the end of 1984 the drop in oil prices affected the ability of foreign customers to build, and layoffs started. "I had no foresight, figured I'd survive; that any day a big job would come in and turn the place around."

The day the bad news came he was actually expecting a promotion. Instead, he and a colleague were told that two departments were being consolidated and both employees would have to go. Stanley had been there for fourteen years. He remained unemployed for a year and a half.

> Life stops for you. At first everyone pats you on the back. Then they start avoiding you; they don't want to hear hard luck stories. Relatives mean well, but you get supersensitive and read things into their remarks. One of them said, "It's better to work for $4 an hour than not at all." Easy for him to say that, he makes $40,000. They'd suggest selling pots and pans in a department store. It's not my line of work.

Unlike Norman, Stanley had a margin of financial security. His wife works part-time, and he is covered by her health insurance. Two of his six children still live at home and contribute toward their room and board. He owns a two-family house, and the tenant's rent covers the mortgage payments. He does his own house and car repairs.

For more than a year he answered ads and visited the state employment service. An employment counselor whom he consulted at $50 an hour advised him to go back to school to learn computerized purchasing, He might have done so, had he not been so close to a job on more than one occasion.

He was one of nine, out of 100 applicants, to be called to interview for a job as purchasing agent for a television station in October 1985. His second interview lasted two-and-a-half hours. "In the end the other fellow got it. You have everything we want except buying electronic components, they told me." He had a second close miss at a purchasing agent job for a small town in the Boston area a few months later.

In March 1986, when he was 55 and almost desperate, he was again one of two finalists, and he made it. He is now on contract to the state as a purchasing agent, earning $22,000, about the same pay as his last salary, but he earns no benefits.

True Grit

Grover B., 58, was the recipient of a golden handshake in the form of six months' pay and a year's health insurance when his job as comptroller in a textile firm folded in April 1984. At that time it seemed pretty good.

> I was sure I'd have another job within a month. It took a year. Six months passed before I realized something was wrong, something I couldn't put my finger on. I'd get called for an interview, very pleasant, nothing happened. Family and friends told me about agencies helping people over 55. I ignored them. They're not talking about me, I said. I've got education, training, background.
>
> Finally I called one at the beginning of 1985. I met with an older man who was very pleasant, sympathetic, understanding, knew my problem. At one meeting with him and another man from the agency, they persuaded me that maybe it was a mistake to hold out for the same money I used to get.

At about the same time he attended a meeting on older workers' problems that he saw advertised in the paper.

> Hire the elderly was the message. I sent my resume and a cover letter to all the business people who spoke about how good the old were, at least six of the companies represented at the meeting. I never even got an acknowledgement.
>
> In May 1985 I took a $15,000 job as a billing clerk. I hadn't typed in forty years but I was happy to get back to work and not go to the unemployment office and placement bureaus.

Four months later he was promoted to accountant.

> I asked for the job. It pays $19,000 and it's better work.
> I never used a computer before and I'm teaching my-
> self. It's very challenging; I enjoy it. But it won't be a
> happy ending until I get back up the ladder to where I
> was.

Temporary Respite

Both Janice I. and Laura T. took temporary office
jobs to keep them going while they searched for positions that would match their last ones. Both stuck to
their determination to find something in their fields
without taking a substantial cut in income.

Janice left her job as managing editor for a small
publisher after the firm was taken over by a large company.

> They threw me out of my office once too often. They
> wanted it for themselves. To me it was symptomatic of
> the whole way the place was being run. I loved the job,
> but I decided it was time to take a stand. They did try
> to persuade me to stay, but they didn't exactly get
> down on their hands and knees. They didn't replace
> me; just divided up the work, and a lot of it doesn't get
> done.
>
> I sent out about 100 resumes, and I got answers to
> most. I came from a well-known press, and I had two
> letters from former colleagues saying I was the great-
> est thing since white bread. I called all the publishers
> in the area, but I didn't have the clout some people
> have. It was a question of slogging around.

A month of "slogging" produced questions like,
"Could you work with younger people," and "Do you
have stamina?" Some people said they would love to

have her. When she made clear she wouldn't accept less than $25,000, they decided she was too expensive.

> I support myself, and I can't afford to work for less. After a month or so, I took a temporary job, typing and so on. It paid $7 an hour. I didn't have word processing, so I really just bumbled around. I got used to the Wang, and they would have liked me to stay permanently. But I wanted to be free to look for a job. They couldn't have been nicer. They let me use their phone and gave me time off for interviews.

After eight months of searching Janice landed an editor's position with a nonprofit institution at her former pay.

> I think they would have preferred that I know a little more about production, but now I'm doing it. I took a chance, but you have to believe in your luck. I was fortunate that I had no dependents, just an old cat.

Laura T, 58 and divorced, is a director of office automation. She had built up a several-million-dollar-a-year word processing operation for a temporary personnel service when she was fired overnight. He boss told her they intended to abolish her job.

> It was such hypocrisy. He said the division had lost money, which wasn't true. My salary had gotten quite large. I was earning $25,000 plus commissions, and was making as much as $50,000. What an honorable person would have done would have been to renegotiate the contract, reduce the percentage of the commission after a certain amount. But he thought now that the operation was all built up he could save a large amount of money by turning it over to the head of another division. He was breaking the contract, and I

might have sued and won. But I wasn't in a position to do that.

At first Laura enjoyed the holiday, but after six months her unemployment benefits ended.

I went on numerous interviews, looking for the equivalent of branch manager. In many instances I would be seen by a man of about 32, and I knew automatically I was not going to get another interview. You just know. It's not only that they don't want older people around. They don't want to pay the money and the pensions.

I have secretarial skills, and when I went to a temporary agency I got jobs instantaneously. I could have gotten a permanent full-time job anywhere I went, because they are looking for the skills plus the stability and the maturity and that stuff. But they don't want to pay for it. Those of us who have word processing skills get $13 to $14 an hour in New York. That can be OK, but it's not at my age and coming from a managerial background. That's where a lot of older managerial women have problems. It's not that you can't have a job. But if you're looking in the $30,000–$50,000 range, forget it.

At the end of a year she duplicated her former post, but with a much smaller temporary personnel service and at a base salary of $30,000. It will take her some time to build up to her previous commission earnings.

I actually answered an ad for a different job, but they had been thinking about starting something like what I was doing. And when they heard my background, we just put it all together.

What I do is a combination of sales and placement. My mandate is to build up a word processing operation for companies that didn't have one before. We help them figure out what they need, we supply temporary help, and we also provide some training.

The temporary industry is a good industry for women to engage in because the companies in it are small and they are not heavily age oriented.

Trying to Rise

Irene B. was one of the few women we talked to whose problem was not job loss but how to start a professional career when she was over 50. She prepared herself by taking an associate degree in social work and completing her BS when she was 51. In 1984, when she was 54, she was a part-time outreach worker for a state-supported elder services agency. Her job was to visit seniors who were receiving home-delivered meals and to encourage them, where possible, to come out and eat at the nutrition center where they would have more social contact.

She wanted to continue working with the elderly. Because she was divorced and two of her three children were still living at home, she also wanted better money. The next step would be case manager, which involved supervising all the home services to elderly clients. It paid $14,500 a year. As she had a BS and an associate degree in social work, she felt she was well prepared.

> I applied three times for openings. The first time they interviewed me and I got a letter saying that there were better qualified people. I called the woman I had spoken to, and asked her just exactly what they were looking for. She said, I would definitely encourage you to apply again when you have a little more experience.
>
> Several months later I did apply again, but I didn't get an interview, or even a letter. The third time I heard nothing either, so I called and spoke to one of

the women who had interviewed me earlier. I said, I feel that I am being discriminated against because I know that the agency has been hiring young women straight out of college. I attended a workshop with one, and she told me that the only experience she had had with the elderly was shoveling snow for an older neighbor. The woman said she didn't feel she had to answer to me, and that was that.

Shortly thereafter, in June 1985, Irene found a job as case manager with another nonprofit senior home-care agency. In February 1986 she enrolled in a master's program in gerontology, studying at night and traveling one weekend a month to an out-of-state university for lectures and consultation. She hopes to move up to supervisor, but she realizes it won't be easy.

When I was hired, the affirmative action officer told me that they encourage older people, that they would love to hire them, but that they don't apply.

That's ironic, because there are people in their 40s and 50s working here who are applying for better jobs in the organization and just not getting them. The places are going to young women almost directly out of college. There are black and Hispanic women who have worked in the organization five, six and seven years and can't move up. There is a joke in the agency that to be a supervisor you have to be white, under 30, and very thin.

I have two women who sit in back of me who are case managers who look as though they were in their early 60s. We have forty-three case managers, and I think those two and I are the oldest. One of the older case managers applied for a new outreach job as homeless coordinator that pays $20,000, but she didn't get it. They hired a younger person.

I do like my job very much, and I'm hoping these things will change soon. All of us case workers have got together and voted to join the Social Workers

Union. The administration was afraid it would spoil our image as one big happy family, but in fact we're not one. The turnover is high. We're looking forward not only to a more lucrative contract but to fairer hiring practices.

Jumping the Gun

Teresa N. and Valerie P., like Janice I., were among those who anticipated fate, went out to meet it.

"When I was 49, something in my head told me I'd better make a change," Teresa told us. "It was now or never."

Until then she had let events carry her. At 37 she had felt her children were old enough for her to return to teaching. She won a fellowship to start on her Ph.D., while holding down a part-time job at a small college. Three years later the realities had changed. Her husband divorced her after eighteen years of marriage; her children were away at school; she could no longer afford to study. She then spent three years teaching full-time at a prep school, which convinced her that teaching adolescents was not her vocation.

The next two years, spent job hunting, destroyed her self-confidence and made her feel that time was running out. She had taken a course in technical writing, had sold articles when she was still at home, and was considered a good financial writer. Her experiences looking for a public relations job opened her eyes.

> I would get interviews, show them my clips. They'd look at them and at my white hair and motherly girth. It was as though they couldn't believe someone like me was still walking around. It suddenly dawned on me that they were the age of my children.

More drastic measures were needed, so Teresa enrolled in an internship program for women who want to re-enter the work force or change positions. It was expensive, but the four-month internship she obtained at a large company changed her future.

> They were understaffed, got used to me, and kept me on from month to month as a contract worker at $1500. I decided I had to get them to give me a permanent job. I understudied everybody, did everything. I even ghost-wrote the memoirs of the widow of a former executive.
>
> Another woman there in her early 50s, Sarah, had had a hard time getting her job, and she became my mentor. The young men were reacting to me as though I were their mother, and they were all just recovering from their mothers. I was proud of my white hair, but I dyed it and I lost weight. When I finally had to leave, they gave me three farewell parties. Sarah insisted that I go to an employment agency; meanwhile she kept my name in front of the manager of the department where I had worked.
>
> I did get a job with a consulting firm, but in the spring of 1984 I was hired back by the company at a salary of $21,400. Since then I've been raised to $25,000. At first my performance was rated D. I had trouble focusing my leads, and I was too slow, but I never missed a deadline. I went to personnel and fought it. You have to fight, and you have to be intensely interested in your work.
>
> I gave up on a promotion, though. I know I'm underpaid, and I won't get recognition. A younger woman, whom I like and respect, has come in at $35,000. You have to ask yourself, what do you really want, to prove your point or to keep the job? Agism is subtle. My boss often says, "After all, you're not 19." I'm vulnerable, replaceable.

Valerie P. dug in her heels. She had a lot to lose. She had been managing editor of a technical journal for ten years and was earning upward of $40,000. She solicited articles on a wide variety of subjects, helped the author think it through, and edited the final result. "I have a knack for drawing out people's ideas," she says. She had succeeded in getting raises and a promotion and, at 61, felt her job was secure, until a new chief editor was named in the fall of 1985.

An autocrat. "We're not going to have any experts around here," he told me. Then he said: "Some people tell me your manuscript commentaries aren't as helpful as they should be." I said "Really? Who? Which manuscripts?" He couldn't say.

On another occasion it was, "You're not going to like working here." Then, a few weeks later: "Have you thought about what I said? I'm not going to kick the old lady downstairs!" He was talking about the old Jimmy Cagney movie where he kicked his mother down the stairs. He meant he wasn't going to do something that would get sympathy for me and make him the bad guy. He was expecting me to quit.

I went to a higher-up. He hit the ceiling and wanted my permission to tell the big boss, but I refused. I decided to fight it myself.

Valerie was not the only older professional at the journal in the line of fire. The executive editor, who was eight months from retirement, was under pressure to quit—until he hired a lawyer. When the pressure stopped, so did the work. He spent the day doing crossword puzzles. The second executive editor, who was 62, was also being pushed to leave.

I went to see my former boss who said, "Don't take things so personally. You have a tendency to look on the dark side." I knew there was a group of younger people who had been trying to move up for years, and they were nibbling at our heels. They were calling us incompetent, and the chorus was getting louder and louder. The new boss promoted young guys, but good managers are few and far between. And they were not any better at human relations, which is a critical skill for this work.

The new boss gave everyone but me and three guys titles and he suddenly left us out of the weekly meetings to choose manuscripts. It was very bad for morale; the others thought, if this could happen to us, it could happen to them.

I kept out of his way, but one day I couldn't avoid him. He said, "You mentioned you were worried about your pension. I've been told it doesn't make all that much difference if you retire early." So I inquired. In fact, the difference is 10% for every year you're short of retirement age.

Valerie kept a record of everything that happened. She also started immediately looking for another job, contacting authors with whom she had worked and other connections in related fields. She had several apparently successful interviews, but nothing came of them, whether because of her age or because she was holding out for a salary between $40,000 and $50,000 a year she could not be sure.

She also sought informal advice from people who had expert knowledge of employment problems. One career counselor, to whom she was sent by a friend, was particularly helpful, confirming her belief that her employer's behavior was not only reprehensible but illegal, counseling her not to let down her guard and not to let herself be pushed out.

After half a year of search she discovered an opening with another technical journal published by her employer. She had two promising interviews, but the salary was considerably lower than she was earning. She was told by management that her current journal would make up the difference, but she was too wary to accept this until she got it in writing.

In the midst of these negotiations, my boss called me into his office and said: "I just thought I'd tell you I think you're handling things so well. I wanted you to know how great you're being." About what? I didn't ask. I just smiled and said well, I always try to do my best. As he continued to pay me compliments, I made my way to the door.

Valerie got the job. Her salary is supplemented by her former journal through an internal administrative arrangement. Although she confesses she often felt close to nervous collapse, she didn't quit, she didn't blow her top. She continued to do her job and, without waiting to be fired, took steps to locate a new one. She also sought expert advice. Most important, but strictly fortuitous, her employer had just been roasted in the local paper for bad personnel policies, and probably did not want to risk more bad publicity in the form of a lawsuit.

■ ■ ■

Throughout this book, and in the last four chapters particularly, we have presented case histories that illustrate the situations in which older workers find themselves. No two stories are quite alike, and no one way of dealing with job loss or the difficulties of remaining in the work force after age 50 is right for everyone. There are some effective general strategies that emerge, however. We turn to these in the final chapter.

10 | REMEDIES AND REFORMS

"**A**s a society, Americans attribute noble qualities to work," declares a report to the government by the Secretary of Labor's Task Force on Economic Adjustment and Worker Dislocation. Issued in the last days of 1986, it continues: "We feel a humanitarian responsibility to help those who are able to work to be suitably employed. We also know that it is in the national interest to keep able workers engaged in productive endeavors. While we recognize that some worker dislocation is going to occur, we must take steps to avoid unnecessary hardship and waste of human capital."

That is a noble sentiment to which the natural response is: Amen. The evidence suggests, however, that this is not the response of the corporate world. Only a few weeks after the Labor Department's report was delivered, the *New York Times* (January 25, 1987) published an analysis in its business section of an emerging ethic from which all traces of concern for the individual or the community has been eliminated.

The turmoil in corporate America, writes the *Times*, "has produced a generation of ruthless management. . . . The new order eschews loyalty to workers, products, corporate structure, businesses, factories, communities, even the nation. All such allegiances are viewed as expendable under the new rules. With survival at stake, only market leadership, strong profits and a high stock price can be allowed to matter."

As we have documented in this book, mid-level personnel reduction has been part of this how-to-succeed-in-business strategy throughout the past decade. It was not, as some of the men and women we interviewed seemed to think, the result of individual employer panic in the face of dwindling sales, but a systematically developed method for more cost-efficient management which has been the subject of field studies by the country's most respected schools of business administration.

A workshop for business leaders and economists held in February 1985, for example, sponsored by the Career Center, a research arm of Columbia University's Graduate School of Business, "was initiated and intended to focus exclusively on corporate resizing efforts aimed at tightening organizational structures, particularly through reductions in managerial, professional and technical personnel," according to the research report on the proceedings.

All this suggests that the trend will continue unabated, and that midlevel jobs will become increasingly scarce. Jobs in domestic manufacturing will decline; production will be exported to cheap labor areas; services will increasingly distribute tasks formerly done by managerial, professional, and technical staff to lower level workers or contract out operations to part-time and temporary personnel. The experiences of our interviewees show how age increases vulnerability to employee reductions and decreases the chances of obtaining one of the dwindling supply of positions in private enterprise.

Changes in national priorities and policies must address the overriding problem of insufficient job opportunity in the for-profit sector. Better jobs for people of all ages are needed and could be created by government and private investment in decent and affordable housing, transportation, protection of the environment, child care, education, and many other essential areas that are now neglected. This would require a major policy commitment to full employment and expanded job training.

Right now no initiatives strong enough to steer such a course are at hand. Until the "waste of human capital"—to use the Department of Labor's expression—is taken seriously, older people will have to rely on less far-reaching changes to improve their prospects.

This chapter suggests some of the efforts that could be made within the limits of present reality. It outlines ways older people can help themselves, policies and practices the agencies that help them might consider, and steps employers and government could take. Our proposals are based on what we have learned by listening to older workers discuss their problems. We offer no magic formulas, but we believe that there are ways of brightening the grey horizons now facing so many hardworking people.

Prudent Precautions

Remember some simple sounding but often neglected precepts.

Keep your records straight. Every employed person should have their career credentials in order at all times, since it is impossible to anticipate when they will be needed. Many interviewees discovered too late that copies of their job performance records, notice of dismissal, and other documentary evidence of their employment history and when and why it ended, were needed to obtain unemployment benefits, assistance from antidiscrimination agencies, or access to a new position.

If you are now employed, make copies of the papers in your personnel files and any communications you receive in the future from management about your work. If you are out of work, you may be out of luck when you try to obtain copies from your last employer. But write and ask for them anyway, by registered mail, with return receipt requested. Your former employer may oblige. If not, a dated copy of your letter and the receipt for it will at least indicate that you have nothing to hide even if your employer does.

It is a good idea to make a note of any discriminatory words or acts directed at you immediately after they happen. A personal record with dates and details of what occurred can be very helpful to you in seeking help or information from an agency or a private lawyer, should you decide to take legal action at any time in the future.

Know your rights. Every older person should be aware that she or he is protected from age discrimination in employment by law. They should know how to obtain help from antidiscrimination agencies, not wait to find out until they feel their rights have been violated. Information about complaint procedures and deadlines can be obtained from the Equal Employment Opportunities Commission office in your area, and from the state antidiscrimination agency, which most states now have.

The public and nonprofit agencies serving older job seekers do not offer such advice, although they well could—a point to which we return. Local bar associations and civil rights organizations are also good places to turn.

Among the best resources are two membership organizations representing older people, the American Association of Retired Persons (AARP) and the Older Women's League. Both offer easy to understand material on the legal rights of older workers and how to go about seeking redress, as well as on many other work and income-related issues. Joining and working with one or both of these organizations is one of the most effective precautionary measures you can take. They work for public policies and legislation to improve training and employment opportunities and pension equity. The AARP also engages in court actions. Their addresses are given in the box on pages 96–97.

Gearing up for the Search

Learn about your career options. People no longer spend their lives working for one or two employers. Today companies change hands and people change jobs every few years, often without advance notice. Most people have a narrow career perspective, based on their daily experience and contacts at work. Learning about major developments outside your orbit can improve your ability to handle change.

Keeping abreast of opportunities in your field or a field that interests you is especially important for older people who have not looked for a job in many years. The best time to start broadening your outlook is while you are employed.

Begin with the easiest task, reading. Public libraries have pamphlets, periodicals, books about the current and projected demand for workers, the qualifications required, and other relevant information. These give the national overview; most state employment services publish data about local conditions and projections.

Talk to people whose business it is to know. Use the career counseling resources that exist in or near almost every community to explore your interests and options. There is no need to pay commercial career-counseling agencies exorbitant prices for unexceptional service. The career education we outline here costs a few hundred, not several thousand, dollars.

These are services sponsored by such nonprofit organizations as YM/YWCAs and community colleges. They offer one-to-one counseling by professionally qualified personnel for $35–$50 an hour, moderately priced workshops and conferences about the realities of various careers, featuring people who speak from personal experience, and seminars on job-related issues.

Most of their programs are designed for people of all ages, and many were started to help women trying to re-enter the work force or move up in it. The assistance they give is essentially unisex, however, and men can profit as well as women.

These services do not give direct referrals to job openings. That is the business of employment agencies. Career counseling and education programs are limited to providing information, advice, ideas and contacts that can make the job search more productive.

To find these programs, call your local colleges and community agencies. If they do not sponsor programs, they will probably know who does. The Yellow Pages may include nonprofit as well as for-profit listings under "counseling" or "vocational guidance." The United Fund agency will know which is which and may have additional suggestions. A telephone call will get you details of activities and put you on the mailing list to receive program notices.

The self-designed, self-administered minicurriculum we suggest here takes only a few hours a month for several months each year, and is well worth undertaking even if you are not currently job hunting. It may produce bad news. Openings in your specialty may be few and far between, plentiful elsewhere, but scarce in your area. You may discover that you need computer skills or other training to stay in the field. It is better to learn what you are up against this way than through time-consuming, frustrating job searching.

Some good news is bound to come out of such career education. You may learn about low-cost courses you can take to update your skills, or expansion taking place in fields related to your expertise. The most valuable product, guaranteed to pay off, will be the contacts you make at workshops and other group sessions.

Most people get jobs through people they know. The more people you turn to, the better the chance of finding the job you want. They will not provide the job, but they offer the stepping stones that may lead you to one.

Building a card file of contacts should be a continuing process that starts now, whether you are looking or not. The file should start off with the names, addresses, business and home telephone numbers of friends, relatives, former colleagues, bosses, customers, neighbors, doctors, lawyers, and expand it as you make new contacts through career counseling programs.

Job-Hunting Strategies

Everyone needs productive personal meetings. Conventional job-search methods provide very few. The unemployed job searcher is alone most of the time, reading ads, writing letters, traveling to employment agencies. Anxiety-producing job interviews are often the only human encounters. A steady diet of these, ending in rejections, can kill the appetite for talking to anyone about employment. Job seekers cut back on contacts to avoid more ego damage; this in turn diminishes their chances of finding an opening, and leads to further withdrawal.

Connecting early and often with public and non-profit agencies of the kind we have described can break the cycle or prevent it from starting. In addition to the programs mentioned above, some agencies offer support groups for job seekers. Join one if you have the opportunity.

As we have illustrated in Chapter Four, support group members help each other by discussing their problems and how they cope with them. Knowing that other people with training, experience, and achievements under their belt are in a situation similar to yours is of itself reassuring. Their suggestions and contacts can be helpful.

Some agencies may (and more should) offer training in networking, using the "information interviewing" technique, also described in Chapter Four. This is an information-gathering interview, as opposed to a job interview, and is a disarming method of obtaining job leads without asking for them.

By talking—by phone, or in person—with knowledgeable people in your field or with possible connections to it, and making clear that you are asking for information only and not for a job, you can often learn what the employment prospects are, and what specifically employers are looking for. With tactful questioning, the job seeker usually elicits concrete advice, and the names of other people to call.

The strategy is time consuming; but in contrast to job interviews, it is nonthreatening for both sides and may be stimulating and enjoyable. It is not likely to produce an actual opening. But it often provides insights, ideas about avenues to explore, and other contacts that can lead to a job. Most important, it strengthens the seeker's will to stay in circulation and continue the search.

Resource Development

The nonprofit career services we have talked about are low-budget operations, financed by user fees and sponsoring institutions. With support from employers, many could provide just as good and perhaps better outplacement service, at considerably less cost, than that proffered by for-profit agencies. If this possibility were to be given consideration by agencies and the business world, many more companies could make outplacement available to many more no-fault job losers.

Local offices of state employment services sometimes offer workshops on job-finding techniques, and some staffs counsel job seekers about career options. They could do much more at very little cost with the cooperation of local businesses, including regular seminars by managers and professionals in various career fields, workshops on age discrimination, training in networking and information interviewing.

The state employment services and some nonprofit groups also provide job referrals for older people, but their help to mid-level clients is very limited. One reason is that government grants, the major source of funds for most nonprofit agencies, are limited to groups serving low-income people over age 55. But there are no such restrictions on the state employment services, and part of the nonprofit agencies' support comes from foundations and other private sources that do not impose such rules.

How to develop more effective assistance that the agency and the people it serves can *afford* is the issue.

Here are a few ideas, again based on the experiences reported by the older workers we interviewed.

Add older workers to the staff. Employing "indigenous" staff has been the policy at agencies serving women and minorities for years. Men and women who have had age-related job problems can be hired as employees or consultants, workshop leaders, support group facilitators, and in other roles. Those few interviewees who received the assistance of such personnel praised their services. They understand the client's problems; offer advice based on experience; and often have expertise in public relations, marketing, human services, and other fields related to the agency's goals.

Educate younger staff who deal with older workers concerning the economic and institutional barriers to employment that their clients face. Most people are not aware of these realities, and agency staff are no exception. Insensitive treatment by younger agency staff was frequently mentioned by interviewees.

The references given at the end of this book cover the facts and figures about the work world situation of older men and women. The clients themselves can provide the rest of the curriculum. Invitations to older workers to discuss their experiences, ideas, and insights with staff could produce material that would enhance an agency's effectiveness. They would also demonstrate the agency's respect for its clients and help to bolster their self-confidence.

Agencies can offer new or revised services without straining their budgets. Most offer training in job-interviewing skills, for example. But the problem for older mid-level workers is how to get more interviews for appropriate openings; and networking using "information interviews" has proved to be an effective method. Training in this technique could easily be added to an agency's program or substituted for job-interviewing workshops.

Few agencies we know of offer basic information or advice concerning age discrimination. Yet interviewees reported coming up against it in their search time and time again. Information on what constitutes discrimination and what can be done about it could be provided to staff and clients at very little cost through workshops led by lawyers and other experts, as a public service or for a very low fee. Bar associations, law schools, civil rights groups, and antidiscrimination agencies would certainly be willing to cooperate.

Helping People Help Themselves

Developing support groups and other ways for older job seekers to meet each other and share problems and ideas, is a most effective agency service. Managers and other professionals who joined such groups told us that they appreciated the understanding and feedback from their peers. They would have been glad to have a more concrete picture of local possibilities for career development, and less of the self-assessment and other introspective exercises which now form the core of many agency sponsored groups.

What they could have used was information on the availability of training programs; the agendas of specialized agencies (recruiting for contract and other part-time professional positions, for example); the identity of companies with direct sales operations and how to evaluate them; the sources of free or low-fee technical assistance for would-be entrepreneurs; and facts about job opportunities in government. Gathering such material takes time, and time is money. Clients could help staff collect the information, and once on hand it can be used by everyone served by the agency.

Perhaps the most effective service a helping agency could provide would be a modest version of the facilities offered by an outplacement service. Searching in isolation, using one's home or a telephone booth or a building lobby as a base, has a devastating effect on job seekers. Those of our interviewees who conducted their search in the supportive physical and social environment provided by a good outplacement service reported a positive experience.

All an agency needs is a small facility for active job seekers to use as a base, offering cubicles for privacy, telephones, desks, word processing and copying equipment or easy access to them, and space for small group gatherings. If several agencies joined and obtained support from foundations and other donors to establish the premises, fees from users and their former employers would cover operating expenses.

Career and employment services, nonprofit and public, can develop other low-budget programs to promote mid-level opportunities, and at the same time help to air the problem of wasted human resources. Job fairs devoted exclusively to older applicants looking for mangerial, professional, and technical jobs would be a challenging project. If the sponsoring agency succeeds in getting employers to participate, clients would benefit immediately. If employers are reluctant, the agency can attract media coverage to the problem and heighten public awareness. Another method of informing the public is to hold public hearings and conferences on the problems of job loss and age discrimination for mid-level older people.

Agencies might also consider sponsoring short-term courses in such subjects as computer literacy, direct sales techniques, computer-aided design, or how to develop a business plan, if such courses are not already available in the community. If the agency can supply the space, client fees could cover the cost of equipment and instructors.

We are convinced that one important component that can add to the success of every agency's endeavor to help mid-level older workers re-enter the job market is the involvement of older workers themselves in the design and delivery of programs. And that is within every agency's budget.

Institutional Change Must Come

Self-help strategies and helping agencies can reduce some of the damage to job losers and their families, but however effective, these are only patchwork repairs. Initiatives by employers and government are required to make a significant impact on the problems our interviewees and so many other older workers face.

Calls for institutional action have already been heard. Recently some leaders in business, government, and academic circles have proposed that employers and government take measures to compensate employees of all ages who lose jobs in downsizing, plant closings, and layoffs. These include training and job-finding assistance.

The report on the Columbia Business School workshop for corporate leaders and economists, quoted at the beginning of this chapter, declares that the success of employer efforts to downsize management, professional, and technical ranks "will depend in large measure on how well they [employers] plan the several stages and on the resources they make available in the form of money and supports to ease the pain of those who must be separated."

It suggests "reassigning surplus personnel to positions in other units of the organization, with or without retraining; assisting them to become retrained to improve their opportunities for jobs with other employers, providing middle and high-level managers with outplacement help and all other forms of retraining and assistance."

The 1986 report of The Task Force on Employment and Aging, convened by The Brookdale Foundation and The Community Council of Greater New York, identifies training, planning for career change, and "creation of varied employment roles" for older workers, as the "three areas in which business can take an initiative today." The published report presents dozens of useful suggestions for employers and government.

They include "reviewing the feasibility of allowing individual and corporate tax deductions for 'career-relevant' educational expenses," not just for job-relevant education and training, the narrower concept articulated in current Internal Revenue Service policy. The report also suggests government-backed retraining loans to job losers, modeled after the student loan program, with payments due when the recipient returns to the work force.

Requiring "age audit" reports from public, for-profit, and nonprofit employment agencies that refer people for temporary or full-time jobs, another suggestion, would discourage age discrimination. The audit would show the proportion of older workers referred and placed. "Because these are activities licensed by the state, review of their performance should be easy," the report states. "Indeed, some minimal level may be defined as a condition for recertification."

The most extensive analysis and the most significant recommendations come from the U.S. Secretary of Labor's Task Force, an independent study group of experts from government, industry, labor, and research. The Task Force spent a year reviewing studies of "displaced workers" and developing proposals to meet their needs.

The women and men whose stories are told in this book are part of the "displaced worker" population, although only a small fraction of it. According to the Task Force, which uses the federal government's definition: "Displaced workers are those who lost their jobs due to plant closings, slack work or [because their] position or job was abolished, and who had significant attachment to their former position [at least three years' tenure]."

Government surveys show that 5.1 million workers were displaced between 1979 and 1984, and another 5 million between 1981 and 1986.

"Frequently the jobs lost have been achieved after working many years for a single employer, and workers have difficulty in finding jobs that pay as much at the outset, or are comparable in other ways," states the Task Force report. "Responses to worker dislocation from both government and the private sector have been spotty and narrowly focused, and the U.S. lacks a comprehensive, coordinated strategy to deal with the problem."

The strategy proposed is to establish "new institutional mechanisms . . . as part of the nation's employment and training system to meet the needs of dislocated workers, including those workers covered by existing programs." The report goes on: "The problem is of sufficient magnitude and urgency that it demands an effective coordinated response with special priority by both the public and private sectors."

Action Agenda

While we wait for that coordinated response, there are measures that could be taken immediately. One of these would be to require at least ninety days' advance notice of dismissal to be given employees about to be "displaced," with paid time off for job search and training. Other improvements would be termination pay based on length of service for those who do not qualify for pension benefits, and employer-financed outplacement service, either by nonprofit career agencies or commercial firms.

The effective ending of illegal discrimination against older workers requires no additional legislation and no special funding. Clear directives from top management to all people who make hiring and firing decisions would start the process. Stricter penalties for violation of existing laws would keep the process moving. Reports from employers to antidiscrimination agencies on the number of mid-level openings filled every month with workers over 50 would reinforce top management's efforts to stop cover-ups and scoff-law practices.

Older mid-level managers and professionals have not yet come forward publicly to advocate their own cause. Activism is not their style, as it may be for their children, the baby-boomers who came of age when protest against race discrimination and the Vietnam War were common. The men and women in this book became adults when World War II, the Korean Conflict, and the spirit of the Eisenhower years (1950s) dominated the scene. Traditional values were central. Loyalty to the establishment has been their lifelong creed.

Job-loss and job-search experiences had "radicalized" some of them, but they had not thought about joining forces with other victims and those at risk to voice their problems, develop a platform, lobby for legislation. Until this happens, age barriers to job keeping and job seeking may not yield. But if older people mobilize to challenge job-loss inequities and age discrimination in employment, those who create and perpetuate the problems will face a formidable foe.

In the meantime, individuals continue to make their way despite the system, including Joan and Richard T. a two-career couple who both entered new fields in their

50s. Their jobs require stamina, flexibility, initiative, and other attributes that supposedly shrivel with age. Joan, a dental hygienist for eighteen years before turning 50, became aerobics coordinator at a top-of-the-line physical fitness club. Richard, retired at 55 from an executive position in manufacturing, became senior vice president at a major bank.

After taking her first classes in aerobics at age 50, Joan decided she would like to make a career of it. She obtained certification as an instructor by attending training workshops and began leading one class a week at a tennis club. She approached the club where she was a member about starting a new program for older people who needed a warm-up course in aerobics before they could manage the regular curriculum.

The club bought the idea. Very few members in their 40s had been signing up for beginning aerobics, and those who had usually dropped out. Joan's age was no handicap. On the contrary, it was the opening wedge. An older instructor, teaching a course she designed for late-starters, would encourage and enable members to master basic skills and then handle the regular courses. The course was a success. Joan was given additional work as well as management duties. Her career was flourishing as of March 1986.

So was her spouse's. Richard had received what every older person dreams of getting, an unsolicited, first-rate job offer after he retired as executive vice president of a plastics company.

> I had planned to start or buy a small business. I felt there was not a lot out there for me at 55 in the corporate world. When I got the call from the president of the bank where I had served on an advisory committee for twenty years, offering me the job, I couldn't believe it. I told him once that I was thinking

of retiring. He said that my years of experience in industry would be very useful. I had great respect for the organization and for him and accepted, of course.

When we spoke, he had been at the bank seven months. "I'm happier than I've been in years. The bubble-and-bounce is back. I'm using my experience and my reputation. And that has turned out to be good for the bank, too."

Richard and Joan T. had excellent track records before their mid-life career switch. Both were highly qualified for their new positions. But many people we interviewed had similar capabilities. What they did not have was Joan's and Richard's close connection to an employer who rated their age as an asset, not a liability. It was not luck or a bolt from the blue that gave each of them the opportunity for a stimulating, rewarding job. It was a business executive who knew their talents, recognized their value to the enterprise, wanted them on board. If that could be the rule in the workworld, rather than the exception, society as well as older job seekers would be winners.

BIBLIOGRAPHY

The Age Discrimination in Employment Act Guarantees You Certain Rights. American Association of Retired Persons, Booklet from Workers Equity Department, 1909 K St. N.W., Washington, D.C. 20049.

Age Discrimination Workshop 1985: State and Federal Litigation. New York: Practising Law Institute, 1985.

Brookdale Foundation. *Employment and Aging: A Task Force Report.* New York: The Brookdale Foundation, 1986.

Butler, Robert N., and Gleason, Herbert P., eds. *Productive Aging: Enhancing Vitality in Later Life.* New York: Springer, 1985.

Community Council of Greater New York. *The Older Job Seeker: Recent Research on the Need for Employment and Training Programs.* Newsletter. New York, December 1984.

Danna, Jo. *It's Never Too Late to Start Over.* Briarwood, NY: Palamino Press, 1984.

Doress, Paula Brown, Diana L. Siegel, et al. *Ourselves Growing Older.* New York: Simon & Schuster, 1987.

Employer Attitudes: Implications of an Aging Work Force. New York: William M. Mercer, Inc., 1981.

Frieden, Elaine, and Waring, Louise S. "The Unemployment Problems of the Late Middle Aged in Greater Boston." Manuscript. Boston: Operation Able, 1986.

Friedman, Lawrence M. *Your Time Will Come: The Law of Age Discrimination and Mandatory Retirement.* New York: Russell Sage.

The Future of Older Workers in America: New Options for an Extended Working Life. Scarsdale, NY: Work in America Institute. 1980.

Ginzberg, Eli. *Resizing for Organizational Effectiveness: A Report of A Workshop.* New York: Columbia University School of Business, 1985.

Greenhouse, Steven. "Surge in Prematurely Jobless." *New York Times,* 13 October 1986, p. D1.

Hudner, Karen. "Probable Cause Standard for the Massachusetts Commission Against Discrimination." *The Docket.* 16 (November 1986): 4.

Kessler, Felix. "Managers Without a Company." *Fortune.* 28 October 1985, p. 51.

King, Joseph A. "The War Between the Generations." *Newsweek,* 14 April 1986, pp. 8–9.

Leonard, Frances. *Gray Paper No. 8: Issues for Action.* Older Women's League, 1325 G St. N.W. LLB, Washington, D.C. 20005.

Levy, Frank; Bluestone, Barry; Thurow, Lester; Whitehead, Jr., Ralph; and Faux, Jeff. *Declining American Incomes and Living Standards.* Washington, D.C.: Economic Policy Institute, 1986.

Marshall, Ray. *Work & Women in the 1980s.* Washington, D.C.: Women's Research and Education Institute, 1983.

Mauro, Tony. "Age Bias Charges: Increasing Problem." *Nation's Business,* 11 April 1983, pp. 44–46.

McLaughlin, Mark. "Leaning on Older Workers." *New England Business,* 6 October 1986, p. 25.

National Institute on Aging. *Self-Care and Self-Help Groups for the Elderly: A Directory.* Washington, D.C.: U.S. Government Printing Office.

O'Brien, Robert, and Kline, Richard. "An Rx for Jobs Lost Through Mergers." *New York Times,* 22 February 1987.

Parnes, Herbert S., et al. *Retirement Among American Men.* Lexington, MA: Lexington Books, 1985.

Pifer, Alan, and Bronte, D. Lydia, eds. *The Aging Society.* New York: W.W. Norton, 1986.

Project on National Employment Policy for Older Americans. *Older Worker Employment Comes of Age: Practice and Potential.* Washington, D.C.: National Commission for Employment Policy, 1985.

Prokesch, Steven. "Remaking the American C.E.O." *The New York Times,* 25 January 1987, section 3, p. 1.

Rix, Sara E., *Older Women: The Economics of Aging.* Washington, D.C.: Women's Research and Education Institute, 1984.

Root, Lawrence S. "Corporate Programs for Older Workers," *Aging,* 351 (1985): 12–16.

Schulz, James H. *The Economics of Aging.* Belmont, CA: Wadsworth Publishing Co., 1985.

Secretary of Labor's Task Force on Economic Adjustment and Worker Dislocation. *Economic Adjustment and Worker Dislocation in a Competitive Society.* Washington, D.C.: U.S. Department of Labor, December 1986.

Shaw, Lois B. *Older Women at Work.* Washington, D.C.: Women's Research and Education Institute, 1985.

Sheppard, Harold L., and Rix, Sara E. *The Graying of Working America: The Coming Crisis of Retirement Age Policy.* New York: Free Press, 1977.

Taylor, Paul. "The Coming Conflict as We Soak the Young to Enrich the Old." *The Washington Post,* 5 January 1986.

Thompson, Duane E.; Hauserman, Nancy R.; and Jordan, James L. "Age Discrimination in Reduction-in-Force: The Metamorphosis of McDonnell Douglas Continues." *Industrial Relations Law Journal,* 8 (1986): 46–67.

U. S. Senate Special Committee on Aging. *Aging America: Trends and Projections. 1985–86 Edition.* Washington, D.C.: U.S. Government Printing Office.

———. *Aging and the Work Force: Human Resource Strategies.* Washington, D.C.: U.S. Government Printing Office, 1982.

———. *The Costs of Employing Older Workers.* Washington, D.C.: U.S. Government Printing Office, 1984.

———. *Health and Extended Worklife.* Washington, D.C.: U.S. Government Printing Office, 1985.

———. *Personal Practices for an Aging Work Force: Private-Sector Examples.* Washington, D.C.: U.S. Government Printing Office, 1985.

Weiss, Francine. *Older Women and Job Discrimination: A Primer.* Booklet from the Older Women's League, 1325 G St. N.W. LLB, Washington, D.C. 20005.

Working Age. Bimonthly newsletter free to businesses and organizations interested in employment issues. American Association of Retired Persons, Workers Equity Department, 1909 K St. N.W., Washington, D.C. 20049.

INDEX